SENDEROS

Teaching Spanish in Waldorf Schools

Authors

Elena Forrer
Claudio Salusso
Enid Silvestry

Contributors

Inés Camano
Barbara Flynn
Carmiña Luce
Diamela Wetzel

Translator

Michael Navascués

Published by:
The Association of Waldorf Schools of North America
3911 Bannister Road
Fair Oaks, CA 95628

Title: *Senderos*

Authors: Elena Forrer, Claudio Salusso, Enid Silvestry

Contributors: Inés Camano, Barbara Flynn, Carmiña Luce,
              Diamela Wetzel

Translator: Michael Navascués

Copy-editor and layout: David Mitchell

Proofreaders: The authors

© 2000 By AWSNA

ISBN # 1-888365-29-3

The authors have made every effort to trace owners of copyright material to secure permision to use their material. In some cases it has not been possible to locate the copyright holder. The authors would be pleased to know of any corrections.

Curriculum Series

The Publications Committee of AWSNA is pleased to bring forward this publication as part of its Curriculum Series. The thoughts and ideas represented herein are solely those of the authors and do not necessarily represent any implied criteria set by AWSNA. It is our intention to stimulate as much writing and thinking as possible about our curriculum, including diverse views. Please contact us with feedback on this publication as well as requests for future work.

David S. Mitchell
For the Publications Committee
AWSNA

Table of Contents

Introductory Verse for Classical Language Lessons

To the one who understands the meaning of language,

The world reveals itself in pictures.

To the one who can hear the soul of language,

The world unlocks itself as being.

To the one who experiences the spirit of language,

The world bestows its strength of wisdom.

To the one who can love language,

Language will grant its own power.

So would I turn my heart and mind

To the spirit and soul of the world;

And in my love for the world

Fully experience my Self.

Rudolf Steiner
(Given to Maria Röschl on November 26, 1922)

Acknowledgements

How many hands formed this book? We will never know for certain, and we would not be able to do justice even if we tried. How to acknowledge our patient families who faced the chaos, the endless papers, and who went off to bed in despair? How can we list the colleagues of our respective schools who accommodated their moods to suit our need? Please, can someone tell us the names of the attentive secretaries who never denied us a smile? We must thank them. In this small corner of the world, made of paper and ink, we wish their presence to be tangible. Without them, the riverbed would be dry.

> "I want to give thanks to the divine
> labyrinth of effects and of causes
> for the diversity of creatures
> that form this universe"

Jorge Luis Borges opens with these four lines one of his Poems on Gifts, and attentively he spells out why we are more than we think we are. And now, with your permission, we would like to name names:

The Orange County Waldorf School opened its doors to the first official meeting in which this book was drafted. From them we lifted a tile, which you will find in one of the pages of this book. Another school that was an integral part of the process is the San Francisco Waldorf School, and in more than one aspect: logistical, pedagogical, and financial. Through their efforts we received a grant from AWSNA. We stole a bell from them. And finally, the Marin Waldorf School, for its encouragement and support. From their garden we took a rose bush.

From art to the parts. Once Michael Navascués had translated "Senderos" into English, we sent it to Lynda Smith. An educator at heart and an editor by profession, she edited the translation, with constructive criticism and engaging commentary. From her hands, the book passed into those of David Weber, who took hours from his busy schedule to carefully read all the book in search of discrepancies, loose ends, and pedagogical and philosophical problems. He also supported us unconditionally to make this project possible.

Now, please stop and return to look at the book's cover: Luis Camano, with enthusiasm and a steady hand, designed it. From the moment we first saw it, we all liked it. Let us not forget Katharine Denny-Salusso and Martha Taimuty for their magical hands — this book continued to take shape thanks to their knowledge of computers and their supportive attitude. And without Robyn Brown and Elizabeth Ruben, who worked as personal couriers between two schools for almost a year, we would still be waiting in line at the post office.

Three more names and we are done: Magdalena Coll, the University of California/Berkeley,PhD. in linguistics, who with diligence and enthusiasm, read the manuscript and whose contribution is present in these pages. And, finally, Lilian Autler and Daniel Roose, masters of many languages, who edited and translated small parts of this book with patience and curiosity, maintaining the voice and melody of the original tongue. Justice was done, as attentive readers will notice.

Now, please stand, wherever you are: in the kitchen, the bedroom, a train, the library. All together let us give thanks to the students. There is no need to explain why, there are innumerable reasons and yet there is only one reason.

Prologue

Senderos is a welcome and overdue addition to the growing field of literature on Waldorf education. The result of a collaborative project carried out by a group of experienced teachers, Senderos provides a careful, grade-by-grade discussion of methods, activities, materials, and curriculum for teaching Spanish in Waldorf schools, from first through eighth grades. Equally important is *Senderos*' presentation of the philosophy of foreign language teaching within the framework of Waldorf pedagogy. The book contains many fruitful observations on the relation of the language curriculum to the content and methodology of the class main lesson work. Thus, despite the focus on Spanish, teachers of other languages who wish to broaden their understanding of Waldorf foreign language pedagogy, may find much that is useful here, especially in the first two chapters.

The ideas of Rudolf Steiner, founder of the first Waldorf school in Germany in the 1920's, have inspired a now rapidly expanding, worldwide educational movement. He offered a few clear guidelines for the teaching of foreign languages, which were developed by teachers and can be briefly summarized as follows. Two different languages should be taught to all children from first grade on. For the first three years the languages should be learned orally, through recitation of verses, songs, tongue-twisters, etc., and through the use of rhythmical activities, dramatizations, and brief situational dialogues. Writing and reading are introduced in the fourth grade, based on materials familiar to the students. From the fourth grade on, grammar is presented on a conscious level, as imaginatively as possible, and using inductive methods. Textbooks are banned until middle school years, and then used only very selectively, if at all.

From these principles, Waldorf foreign language teachers have evolved varied programs and lessons that are alive with singing, recitation, movement activities, folklore, poetry, and drama—to which are added elements of geography, art, biography, and so on. The list of cultural activities and materials will depend on the particular creative talents and interests of the teacher, and on the needs of the class—as well as on time constraints.

The first two chapters of *Senderos* offer a detailed perspective of the Waldorf foreign language approach, and the ways in which it dovetails with the broader goals of educating and meeting the needs of the growing child, according to Waldorf pedagogy. Chapter 3 is rich with examples of the imaginative use of activities and materials developed by teachers for specific learning goals. Each activity is aimed at a particular age group, and is designed to engage the student in the language in a living way, avoiding the plodding abstractions of a textbook approach. This chapter concludes with a very useful table outlining grammatical topics by grades. Chapter 4, "Poetry, Dramatization, and Recitation," is a selection of literary and cultural materials, with commentaries on their classroom application. Included are some excellent examples of poetry and dramatizations for grades 1 to 8. Teachers may wish to try some of these in their own classes. Eventually they should be inspired to investigate or create different materials that suit their own particular interest or circumstance, and those of their class. The last chapter contains interesting descriptions of how to incorporate traditional dances and festivals in the Spanish curriculum. The book concludes with two useful bibliographies, one on teaching foreign languages in Waldorf schools, and the other on sources consulted in the creation of *Senderos*.

As the title suggests, *Senderos* takes the reader along a number of paths for the teaching of Spanish to children. It does so with imagination, understanding, and great dedication to the task at hand. Along the way it skillfully interweaves a pertinent discussion of some of the ideas and ideals which inspire Waldorf education. To date, very little has been published in United States on this subject of Waldorf foreign language methods and curriculum. *Senderos* should naturally prove most beneficial to Waldorf teachers of Spanish. It is my hope that the book will also find a wider audience among teachers in other schools, as there is currently in this country a renewed interest in starting foreign language learning at an early age in the elementary schools. Waldorf schools recognized many decades ago the real need for a "natural," oral method of language learning, starting in the first grade, when the imitative capacities and memory of children are still strong and spontaneous. The creative approaches developed by Waldorf language teachers are certainly worthy of closer examination. The publication of *Senderos* is thus a timely event, offering guidance within the Waldorf movement, and the potential for dialogue with other foreign language educators.

Michael Navascués, Ph.D.

Introduction

The words, verses, ideas, and convictions that give voice and shape to this book have traveled countless paths. Paths—senderos—through many different landscapes: friendly, hostile, indifferent, and rigorous. On many occasions these verses have taken on a life of their own and wandered off through the schools, genteel salons. and hallowed halls of learning, like stray dogs during the lull of the afternoon siesta time. At other times, we put them on a leash and paraded them from grade to grade, exposing them to the use and abuse of curious, healthy, diligent students.

In the midst of the unruliness of all this scattered knowledge we decided one summer afternoon in 1997, while gathered on the shores of the Pacific, to create some order out of chaos. With patience, and then with passio, we recited out loud the alphabet of our languages; we tried to enumerate the objects that slumber and dance in our briefcases: whistles, boots, hourglasses, magic wands, hopes, melodies, vexations, puppets, hats, stories without beginnings and stories without endings. And as the sun set into the murmuring waves, we agreed that the time was right to draw a brightly colored map together, a map in which all the roads would lead to the same horizon, and the sunshine of our dedication and experience would illuminate the paths to be followed by other feet as curious as our own. And so, solicitous, stoical and hard pressed, we left behind the Pacific with its poetry of gulls and went home, followed by the distracted stray dogs which, as we well know, are never lost.

That is how *Senderos* was born. through us. more than two years ago. Once the work had been divided among us according to our personal strengths and preferences, we got down to business and began writing, ordering, rearranging, erasing, correcting and drafting each part of the book. This book, at the same time one and many books, was created *ad honorem,* as though our time, patience and decorum were limitless.

Now it is no longer ours, but has a life of its own, and will have to stand on its own merits; and you, gentle or jaded reader, will now be its judge.

Chapter 1

The Mission and Teaching of Foreign Languages in Waldorf Schools

"What is more quickening than light?
A conversation—an encounter through words."

—Goethe

The purpose of the study of languages is to develop the ability to communicate. Through the art of communication, we confront the essence of the other person. This process raises one's social conscience and fosters an important objective of Waldorf education: to cultivate an interest in others, which will inspire students to share their knowledge, abilities, and experiences. Those who are touched by such an interest will contribute to global understanding and to the progress of humanity.

Studying languages is a window into the soul of a culture, into its genius, individuality, and musicality. The manner in which we think is expressed through the language that we speak, and it is well known that learning another language expands one's thoughts and ability to penetrate the feelings and the soul of the other culture. In capturing the spirit of the language that molds human beings, one begins not only to understand other cultures, but also to change one's way of thinking, feeling, and acting.

Although language expresses the thinking of an individual or a culture, it arises from the life of feeling. The language is internalized in the child's feelings, a realm of interplay between sympathy and antipathy, and this process works on the growth of imaginative thinking and the development of the human being.

Foreign languages in Waldorf schools are an integral part of the curriculum. Two languages of different origins are taught in Waldorf schools from first to twelfth grade. Each language satisfies different needs in the child, providing a balance for his or her soul. Each language, with its particular music and rhythm of intonation and articulation, and the structure of its parts, offers a special experience to the child. It is up to each school to determine, in accordance with local circumstances and needs, the languages that are taught.

In Waldorf education our objective is to offer students the opportunity to live in the "genius" of the language. We want them to be able to create brief conversations, to read simple stories, and to write sentences and paragraphs, developing the capacity to think by letting the language penetrate their being. Also, through daily rhythms, repetition, continuity of instruction, concentration, and follow-up, the will of the student is developed. These activities help the individual transform the material to make it her own.

In the upper grades, when the students are more conscious of their own tongue, they discover alternative forms of expressing themselves, whether in prose or verse, and they become more aware of the intricate structures of their own language through study of the grammar, syntax, and idiomatic expressions of the foreign language.

In the workbook *Forming the Lessons of Grades One through Eight*, written for the Pedagogical Section, and published by the Rudolf Steiner College, we find the following reference about the mission of language:

"Through the inner flexibility of their speech organ, the children find their way to a flexibility of soul and an openness that has an effect on their entire later life and especially on their social abilities. The foreign language lesson is suited like practically no other lesson to encourage openness and awaken interest for what is foreign to oneself – and in our time of widespread racism and social conflict on both a small and large scale this is a pedagogical mission of the first order."

General and Specific Objectives for the Teaching of Spanish

1. To sow a seed for the learning of Spanish and develop the ability to communicate in the language.
2. To develop the capacity for understanding and acceptance of the different Spanish-speaking cultures, promoting and generating a feeling of brotherhood among human beings.
3. To discover other points of view, by acquiring the ability to reflect

on aspects of one's own culture.
4. To develop and deepen capacities for thinking, and willing through the Spanish language.
5. To develop supportive learning conditions among several disciplines.
6. To foster the participation of students in local and international multilingual communities.

To realize these general objectives, teachers need to commit themselves to the following:

7. Find pathways for planning, conducting, and teaching their lessons.
8. Find methods and materials in the language, appropriate for the age group, to assist and nurture the child in all his faculties.
9. Offer the living qualities in the language not only through its artistic and literary expressions, but also as an experience of daily living.
10. Be committed to bringing the language to the students with the appropriate correctness and respect, so that its genius and its spirit will be living in the richness and liveliness that are necessary in the class.
11. Find stability and acceptance of the foreign language program within the framework of Waldorf pedagogy.
12. Help the class, through pedagogical methods, find a meaning in what is being taught.
13. Help in the harmonious development of the authority of the teacher in relation to the handling of the class.
14. Establish a clear and open communication with colleagues, class teachers, and subject teachers.
15. Establish a harmonious relationship with one's assigned mentor, receiving the support necessary for the implementation of the program that is being carried out.

Just as necessary as the identification of general objectives is the establishment of specific ones that frame with clarity and precision what we seek to achieve in the areas of thinking, feeling, and willing. These faculties are intimately related and express themselves differently according to the stage of development of the child.

In the first three years of school, the experience of the language is completely oral. Through gesture, mime, songs, poems, rhymes, games, and drama, the child learns vocabulary and, with her powerful capacity for imitation, remains connected with the environment and her practical everyday life. A rich thematic variety is found in nature, colors, the parts of the body, clothing, food, the rooms of a house, numbers, clock time, the family, climate and seasons, the days of the week, and the months of the year. The children also form phrases that become practical expressions, and with recitations rich in lively movements, they eventually form a tapestry of words that one hopes will belong to them.

Grades four and five are transitional, bridges toward the upper grades. What has already been learned by ear is now reviewed and expanded more consciously. Up to this time, the child is more closely connected to nature and the environment, but between the age of nine and eleven, he begins to experience a separation from the environment; he differentiates between himself and his surroundings, while experiencing an increased consciousness of selfhood. The stronger the consciousness of self, the sooner the capacity for imitation diminishes. The child begins to assert himself more and to change attitudes.

In order to bring to the students a stronger awareness of language structure, they are exposed to the first grammatical elements, going "from the whole to the parts" at first, and a little later, to verb conjugation. This analytical activity awakens the child to a greater understanding, as words already used in vocabulary become consciously manipulated in grammar.

In sixth, seventh, and eighth grades, more complex grammar concepts are presented, since these provide important formative elements for the growing capacity of analytical thinking which begins to develop in adolescence. Moreover, the focus on grammar fosters concentration and strengthens the will forces during puberty. The curriculum also continues to develop the powers of imaginative thinking, which are actively reinforced through the use of verses, poems, plays, tongue twisters, songs, history, biographies, and dialogues.

Chapter 2

Spanish and the Waldorf Curriculum

First Grade

The form of the language class is quite similar to that of the main lesson, whose content is organized in a rhythmical flow of "in-breathing" and "out-breathing." Rhythm is essential for 6- and 7-year-olds, inasmuch as the child feels united to the world and the world to him. This rhythm offers him security in facing life and the new experiences that continually appear.

When the language teacher enters the first grade for the first time, the children are waiting expectantly for the lesson, because for them it is a new experience. It is therefore important to create the right mood and timing, just as an orchestra conductor prepares himself for presenting his concert. One needs to prepare a kind of ceremony: from the greeting to the goodbye, every aspect of the lesson has to be a ritual.

For the new language teacher this can be a real challenge, especially if she is not familiar with Waldorf education. Therefore, preparation is absolutely imperative. The teacher has to present prepared material with rhythm and harmony, and ought not to depend on reading notes.

The main-lesson story material of the first grade is primarily fairy tales, which carry an ancient wisdom. They nourish the soul with images of the archetypal battle between good and evil and the soul's development. These ancient tales were passed down orally, to help human souls to find their way in the world. The famous Grimm brothers' fairy tales were compiled between 1812 and 1815. This vast collection of stories creates, among other things, understanding of the development of a culture through its oral and written tradition. There are similar stories found in the folklore of Spain and Hispanic America, passed on by oral tradition. Such tales, whether of Hispanic or Germanic origin, are presented in the early grades of the Spanish class to help guide the moral development of the child, as well as stimulate his imagination or pictorial thinking through the vehicle of another language. The teacher uses this vast and rich world to bring to the class a universe filled with vivid images and dramatic scenes.

Spanish is extremely rich in lyric poetry, and has many examples of lively and imaginative poems suitable for children and adolescents. The teacher should not feel intimidated by the length of a poem, because at this age the capacity for imitation and recitation is at its peak. In time, the children are able to speak that wonderful poetry, and, if the teacher can find the right roles, as well as costumes and props, the class could dramatize with beauty and innocence a chosen work in verse.

It is important for the teacher to present a harmonious repertoire of verses, movements, and rhymes in a systematic way. To do this, he should repeat each activity once or twice during the class and continue this same collection for weeks or months. Then the teacher can start to substitute new songs or verses as the children learn the material.

At the beginning of the class the children stand up and begin to repeat the verses, songs, and movements selected by the teacher. Gestures are important: the children will imitate completely everything that we do. In this regard Rudolf Steiner says that in grades one to three, imaginative imitation is still so strong that the child can absorb the language in its totality, instinctively, by habit. For this reason gesture is particularly important, for it is a continuation of speech. Therefore, speech should be accompanied by an appropriate movement and with real meaning, without exaggeration. Steiner also points out that one need not worry that a child memorizes a poem of 4, 6, 7, or 8 lines, and understands only minimally its content. One can memorize it through the sounds and rhythms, and later understand it. This approach contributes to the acquisition of the language. That is why Steiner emphasizes that in grades one to three, poetry is preferable to prose, which should be kept to a minimum.

Next comes a second phase of the lesson. The children sit down and are prepared to receive a content that requires a greater concentration. This material depends a great deal on the imagination of the teacher, on her creativity, and on her means of expression and presentation. There is great freedom with respect to the planning. One should never translate. One should let the children repeat, answer and ask questions chorally or individually, and insofar as possible, set up dialogues. It is extremely important that the presentation as well as the topic of the material should be clear and simple. The class learns new vocabulary by repeating and observing what is happening: it is recommended that the teacher bring a basket or a "special box" with objects that represent the content that one wishes to teach that day. It is necessary for the material to be related to the child's world, which is inhabited by fairies, elves, queens, and other fairy tale characters.

At the beginning the pupils respond chorally, but little by little the teacher introduces individual questions, especially to the children who are less inhibited and are now ready to respond. Soon brief dialogues can be set up, in which questions about size, color, number, what is missing, what one is holding, etc. are asked. Memory games are also quite appropriate. One can capture attention by bringing scenes to life with sounds, masks, costumes, felt cut-outs, dolls, or other visual aids.

Toward the end of this second part of the lesson the children generally show signs of fatigue. Then it is wise to change the rhythm again with activities such as a circle game, a dance or other movement with hands and feet, such as getting up and sitting down. In this phase there should be more relaxation and less form. Such movement not only helps the soul to incarnate, but also creates a healthy rhythm in the lesson. Indeed, Steiner emphasizes the importance of movement at this early age, when the child is most alive in the will. He says it is important to give the children instructions that are not followed by a reflection or an answer, but rather by an action, which engages the will.

Upon finishing his class, the teacher has taught an extensive content in a rhythmical and natural manner. The teacher again brings this content in the following days, modifying details and/or introducing new things. The material selected should be rich, beautiful, and substantial, from a verse, a short folk song, to a lyric poem of the highest artistic expression. Through such offerings the child enters the soul of a culture, even though he may not yet understand the meaning of what he is repeating. The formative qualities of language enrich the child's feelings, nourishing his soul. Precisely for this reason, it is very important not to translate the material, and especially in the first few grades. If the teacher translates, the language loses its magic and becomes intellectual thought.

At this age the powers of language acquisition are well developed, which is why the teacher has the great opportunity to teach orally without translation. When the child learns to speak for the first time, he begins connecting sounds with objects until he is able to picture the object and repeat its sound. Rudolf Steiner called this "forming a mental image." It is through these mental images that we learn to express thoughts, at first in a simple way and then with more complexity. According to Steiner, a foreign language is learned in a similar way. Little by little, that world of songs, verses, and movements is transformed in later years into rapid learning and a large assimilation, allowing the child to have a total experience of the language.

Rudolf Steiner insists that one should converse in the foreign language from the beginning and provide opportunities for the children to speak. Until the change of teeth at age 6 or 7, the child relates less to meaning and content; rather, he lives in the sound. After the seventh year, he relates to the content, but more to the emotional content rather than the intellectual. Therefore, before the ninth year, the teaching of the foreign language takes place entirely through speaking, so that the child learns in the realm of feeling and imagination.

Second Grade

Just as in first grade, rhythmical organization of the lesson is essential. Perhaps the greatest change in this year lies in the child's growing awareness that language has a social function that it allows for communication. He realizes that there are other people who communicate in a different way. That is why it is important to individualize the dialogues.

The basic story material of the main lesson is fables, legends, and stories of saints. Many of the children have turned eight and begin to "wake up" and to notice that there are differences among human beings. Human characteristics, the defects and virtues, are reflected in the fables, in which animals embody those qualities. The children see these characteristics reflected in a humorous way in the animal world, and by this means they learn to combat their own lower impulses. In Spanish we have important writers of fables. Outstanding ones are Iriarte, Samaniego, and Lope de Vega, whose fables *El consejo de ratones, El burro flautista, En un panal de rica miel,* and *La lechera* are a few examples.

The lives of saints, told alongside the fables, have, of course, a different focus. These biographies reflect a state of transformation as human beings. Their dedication as well as their works are a model of conduct and goodness. Saint Martin of Porres had a most beautiful life, not only because of his social condition as a black man, but also because of his incredible humility and simplicity. Other examples of kindness and virtue are Saint Rosa of Lima, Juan Diego, and the legend of the Virgin of Guadalupe.

The legends of Native Americans reflect the unique relationship between man and the elements. These legends, for example those published by Alma Floor Ada or Lulú Delacré, can be acted out, for they represent a wealth of colorful material.

At this age the child becomes conscious of the function of language among different people. The repetition of dialogues, either chorally or individually, can help a class enormously. If the teacher, once the children are seated, calls on two or three volunteers to respond to a series of questions, this will serve as a review for the others. After this, the teacher can present new lesson material, and then end with a story, a game, or a dramatization of something recited previously in the rhythmical segment.

Third Grade

The third grade continues a format similar to that of the first and second grades, with respect to the distribution of the content of the material during the class. Also, the class continues to be oral from beginning to end. Nevertheless, when Steiner was asked if one ought to allow the child to begin to write in the foreign language in the third grade, he answered that they can begin to write short, easy sentences that express a simple thought.

At times this can turn out to be a difficult year for the language teacher, because the children begin to feel separate from the world. Imitation begins to disappear, and gesture acquires a new importance. If the teacher insists on a presentation based on imitation, she may easily lose control of the class. If the teacher has found a repertory appropriate to the developmental stage of the children, eventually they themselves will begin to repeat the movements out of their individual need for expression, rather than out of sheer imitation. During this year it is extremely important to present educational challenges that will motivate the children, as well as to establish respect and authority toward the teacher. Material that requires concentration and contains humor can help to break the ice between the new teacher and the class.

During third grade the boys and girls listen to the story of the Hebrew people of the Old Testament. The objective is to be able to help the child leave a "group consciousness" in order to find their own individuality—which later is reflected in the arrival of Christ. Because of this, the imitative capacity is diminishing. It is necessary to create a space for the children to generate their own expressions, adding to what they have previously learned. For this purpose it is advisable to present artistic drawings and let the pupils describe the situation. The challenge this year is to form complete sentences. On occasion, one can make a tally of all their correct answers. This kind of individual practice can be presented as a challenge or motivation to the students.

Precisely because of the loss of the children's experience of "paradise" of the earlier years, the Waldorf curriculum welcomes them to the earth. The self, or "I" is in the world, a world in which they have to work, build, plant, and harvest their fruits. The children learn in a practical way about all the activities that unite man to the earth. Farming, trades, domestic chores, the produce of the earth, building, the division of time and measurement, are all important topics taken up during the third grade. This rich content is very advantageous to language teaching, because the teacher can introduce all these themes. The challenge lies in finding ways to bring these subjects to the class. It is advisable to have at hand many drawings, objects, books, and also real materials such as grains, wool, fruit, vegetables, etc., which will help the teacher to form the lesson. The presentations can be longer and more practical than in previous years, although there is a greater loss of fantasy. Dialogue and role-playing are highly useful tools, and instructions to be carried out can be more detailed. It is important to let the children re-tell the stories; the teacher must skillfully lead this practice.

By the end of third grade, the aim is for students to possess a basic vocabulary with which they can answer simple questions with complete sentences, and to understand basic instructions. The teacher will continue to build on these skills in the following years.

Fourth Grade

Fourth grade is a time of change for language teachers. This is when the children learn to read by writing the material that they have memorized in previous years. It is important to begin in a simple manner, with a poem from the first or second grade. It is then very satisfying to observe everything that they remember and the quality of their reading. This re-presenting of material learned previously is essential. By starting to read material with which they are already familiar orally, they will be able to establish a solid basis in their reading. This process also facilitates good pronunciation. Since they have listened to or acted out the reading material previously, the children are able to form a picture of what is happening, without requiring a translation. Thus, writing is the first step toward reading: first the children write in their notebooks the chosen material (at first only four or five lines) and then, chorally, they begin reading the selection aloud with the teacher. At a later time, stories can be copied and distributed for reading aloud and discussing.

In this grade the pupils can also write their first compositions. They can begin in a simple manner with their own descriptions, or the description of a drawing done previously in class. It is important that the students not simply copy the teacher's writing. Rather, they should first form a mental picture of what they are to write in order to be able to recapitulate orally, and as a final step, write the scene in their notebooks.

This year the teacher will begin to lay the foundation for grammar, and this should be connected to life itself. One should not work at an abstract level. Grammatical principles need to be related to real objects in the students' surroundings. At this age there is a need to find one's place, and there is growing awareness of others and the world. The children are trying to establish their individuality, and at this time grammar can help them to find solidity and stability. (These points will be elaborated in the grammar section of Chapter 3.)

As in earlier years, the class begins with songs and verses. During the main lesson the boys and girls hear Scandinavian mythological tales, which are characterized by a strong rhythm in the recitation. It is therefore recommended to choose alliterative and rhythmical material. The stories of El *nabo*, *El hombrecito de mazapán*, *Esta es la casa que Juan construyó*, *Estando la mora en su lugar*, *Las bodas del tío Perico*, represent appropriate material for recitation. The class learns to recite the stories rhythmically, and when they have memorized them, they can be used as material for dramatization. Alliteration is typical of old Nordic literature, and reflects in its expression the human will. Speech that activates the will can help to foster the children's emerging individuality.

At this age the inner life awakens more to external interests. Sometimes this awakening leads toward materialism, or it can manifest as a heartfelt interest in the human being. As the parts of speech are connected to thinking, feeling, and willing, this new interest in the human being sets the stage for the acquisition of grammar. The result is a step toward cognitive awakening. Differentiating all the pronouns, learning basic rules of gender and number, as well as the conjugation of verbs—these processes come into focus starting at this age. In the language class, moreover, the teacher lays the grammatical foundations at the same time as the main lesson teacher. Such parallel work can be a great help and is the fruit of collaboration.

Another aspect of this grade is that the class begins to learn about its environment. Geography lessons satisfy the children's inclination to get to know the land and people around them. Because the main lesson teacher teaches them about maps of their region and state, it is an ideal time for Spanish teachers to introduce names of regions, such as Sierra Nevada, Nevada, Los Ángeles, Los Altos, and many others. For those who live in the Western United States, it is possible to take the students to Hispanic sites in the region. This is an open door for exploring culture, customs, and, finally food, keeping in mind the possibility of a trip where the children, at mealtime, should interact in Spanish at the restaurant.

Fifth Grade

Rudolf Steiner developed a curriculum that fundamentally addresses the growth and development of the child. To arrive at this he studied the development of humanity itself through the ages, and he observed a correlation between the evolution of human consciousness and thinking, and the development of the child. He thus created a curriculum of unparalleled wealth, in which all cultures are reflected for their contribution to the development of humanity. In this grade the students begin learning about the cultures of India, Persia, Mesopotamia, and Egypt, culminating in Greece. The latter culture is essentially one of balance, expressed by the movement of the discus thrower. Fifth graders, too, have achieved a balance in their growth. Physiologically they have not reached puberty—although they are close to it—but they are, for the most part, physically and mentally well balanced.

For the Spanish teacher, this moment of equilibrium brings a greater flexibility in managing the class. The students are found to be more receptive and less likely to argue with the teacher. In general, the lesson uses the same format as in previous years, but some stages are longer. The first stage, the movement stage, is now greatly reduced. The boys and girls do not need to move about as much as the younger ones, for the realm of feeling is experienced more strongly than the will. The beginning of class is the same, though shorter: poetry and songs, oral conjugation or short recitations. After a few minutes, the children sit down, and the teacher can begin asking about previous material. This is "recall," going over the grammar and other material that require greater attention and concentration. Next, one can introduce a new concept or vocabulary item. After this the class can do some writing or go on to reading. It is advisable for the students to have notebooks, which will reflect artistically all of the material being learned. Cultural notes, poetry, and grammar could all be included.

In this year and the following ones, reading acquires great importance. Steiner insists again and again that new vocabulary should be expressed through a context or a composition, not a list of words. The difficulty is to find appropriate reading material that will be simple yet stimulating. Often, stories in which the protagonists are children of their age are the best material. These readings can inspire written questions, syntactical compositions, and study of vocabulary and grammar. In the reading lesson we also focus on recapitulation of what has just been read.

Steiner says that, at this age, children begin to learn better with readers, and it is important to find a book of appropriate, coherent readings. It is good to go over the readings sentence by sentence, as with the younger pupils, the teacher should always speak first. He also adds that one should not translate. One can check if they have understood the reading by having them give, in their native tongue, a "free rendering" of the meaning or content of what has been read. Starting in fourth grade, one needs to move toward translation in the following manner: say something in the native tongue and let the child express it in the second language. It is not advisable to allow them to translate long texts directly into their native language. These methods are used up to sixth grade. Of course, some elements of grammar are already presented in fourth and fifth grades. Prose is a good tool that allows us to work with a text and the grammar at the same time. Finally, Steiner suggests that the children should be allowed to converse as soon as possible.

Because fifth graders view nature more objectively, botany is introduced during the year. Poems about growth and nature are therefore quite appropriate. During this year one can ask, after a recitation, about key words that they already understand. Little by little the class takes in the essence of the poetry, without having to translate. They form mental pictures, and satisfy the desire to understand what they are saying, for they now need to understand through mental pictures what they are repeating.

The teacher has much freedom to choose themes during the year. The legends of Hercules, the Greek hero, are very popular in Spain. They are related to important myths from antiquity in the Iberian Peninsula. Legends of the Incas, who worshipped the sun, are also appropriate, especially in the story of Manco Capaq, which parallels the dynasty of the pharaohs.

Sixth Grade

As the faculty of thinking awakens, the learning of languages undergoes a considerable change. Growing self-awareness means oral presentation of the teacher stops being as accessible to the children as it was in earlier years. The recitations lose vigor, and choral speaking seems like a whisper. Changes reflecting the social relationships of the students begin to appear. A desire to be accepted intensifies, as well as a search for models of behavior. At the same time, new faculties awaken an understanding of cause and effect. As the student begins to show a real desire to communicate his pleasures and preferences in the language classes, the challenge is to find material that will satisfy his growing individuality.

When working with poems or plays, individual recitations can be assigned to different students. Descriptive or epic themes are quite appropriate for this individualization, and can be found in Spanish epic poetry. The *Romancero Español* (old Spanish ballad collection) is very suitable, not only for its historical context, but also because it contains wonderful examples of both epic and lyric styles.

In the course of history, after the great culture of ancient Greece, Roman culture appears in all its vigor. Likewise in the Spanish class, the teacher, if she wishes, can speak of the Roman expansion in Spain, and how in the period of Augustus, Córdoba was one of the greatest cities in the world. Moreover, the subsequent invasion of the barbarians, the arrival of Islam, the Middle Ages, comprise 1,400 years of historical expansion that the main lesson teacher covers during this year.

On the American continent, the culture of Teotihuacán, found in the city of the same name, which later became "City of the Gods," appears in the first centuries after Christ. In its social and civic organization, it shows parallels with Roman culture.

Steiner offers suggestions on the teaching of geography. During the sixth grade the students learn the geography of Europe, and this provides an opportune time for the Spanish teacher to broaden knowledge of Spain. Steiner explains that it is necessary to discuss with joy a country's literature, customs, states of mind; geography should be humorous.

On finishing sixth grade, the student can express himself with a certain degree of grammatical autonomy. He is aware of the conjugation of regular verbs and various irregular verbs in the present tense, as well as other parts of the sentence. He also begins to work on conjugation in the past tenses, even though expression will occur largely in the present, given the complexity of verb endings in Spanish.

Seventh Grade

In this grade the search for answers, causes, and reasons continues. Discoveries are made and new goals are reached. In the main lesson the students learn about the laws that govern the changes in nature and in the human body. The students study how thinking during the Renaissance epoch depends entirely on the human being himself, and not just on the authority of tradition. This leads to a strong feeling of separation from the world. Such objectivity makes possible a deeper study of natural sciences. The spiritual freedom acquired toward the end of the Middle Ages and the beginning of the Renaissance brought a spiritual and cultural struggle that changed the consciousness of humankind. The students also reflect this change. Their new vision of the world needs new perspectives and answers. Likewise, in the language class, they are going to require a content that responds to their needs, as well as new challenges that will support the strengthening of their sense of self.

Students participate in the enthusiasm of knowing about new worlds. The study of voyages and discoveries forms a major part of the main lesson curriculum. For Spanish teachers, it is an extraordinary opportunity to explore old cultures of the American continent. The students' fascination with Teotihuacán, the Aztecs, the Mayans, and the Incas is profound. The presentations are always carried out in Spanish, and if possible, accompanied by photographs or illustrations that help to stimulate understanding. It is also the right time to teach the geography of the Americas. The music of Argentina, Bolivia, Chile, the Caribbean, and many others, are quite appropriate during this grade and the next. Instruments such as a charango, a guitar, maracas, or a drum can enliven the songs tremendously. Learning dances that accompany this music can also be appropriate.

As for poetry, Latin American authors can be chosen. Many poems illustrate the land, the jungle, or the characteristic nature of the region, which can reinforce the geography block. Also appropriate are themes that reflect the quest for self-knowledge, which the student shares. As for narratives, many books carry a historical or legendary content that reveals the great diversity of cultures and influences. Stories of European explorers and conquerers, as well as tales from the oral traditions of indigenous peoples can be used. Such legends and historical narratives can likewise be useful to the presentation of grammar.

In the teaching of grammar, it is important for the teacher to present it within a real context. In seventh grade, there may be various levels among the students, and to attend to each one properly will depend on the resources of the teacher. Ideally, if the students have studied Spanish since first grade with the same teacher, they should have reached a certain level of fluency. A review at the beginning of the year is essential in order to proceed with irregular verb conjugations in the simple past, the imperfect, and the present progressive. Likewise, one needs to stimulate conversation with specific objectives, that is, the ability to respond in different situations with a certain degree of competence.

Eighth Grade

In this grade the main lesson teacher will cover the development of the Industrial Revolution. The students likewise explore the search for independence and cultural and spiritual freedom, which was reflected intellectually in the ideals of the French Revolution. The content of the history classes is clearly marked by the the struggle for independence in the North American colonies, and the new consciousness of freedom and rights. But the students are also interested in the changes in other countries, and in hearing the biographies of heroic people who changed the world, such as Simón Bolívar, José Martí, César Chávez, and others.

In the language class, the students' individualization is reflected in their work. In general, they are able to work with a fair amount of independence, while feeling the need to learn and the desire to communicate. However, if the class has undergone changes in the student body and in teachers, there will most likely be a disparity of levels and motivation. When this happens, consider combining the seventh and eighth grades and form groups according to levels. On the other hand, if there has been continuity within the class, and the main lesson teacher has maintained an adequate academic level, a good attitude toward learning will be reflected in the language class.

Increasingly, in the language class the teacher will shorten the movement part of the lesson, and lengthen work that requires thinking and uses the language in practical ways. The teacher will begin the lesson with a poem or song, and then go on to recapitulation (re-telling) of the previous lesson. This phase may last five to seven minutes. Then the teacher will present new material, connecting it to what was explained previously. Whenever the presentation contains grammar, one should let the students deduce the rule themselves, according to the examples presented. Steiner tells us that this practice in particular helps to strengthen the ego of the students.

The rest of the lesson can be devoted to oral or written practice, reading, and recapitulation of the reading. Working in pairs at this age is not only necessary but beneficial. It is a time-saving method, and creates a space for students to use the language socially, without being under the constant scrutiny of the teacher. The student at this stage has to become responsible for writing down and understanding the assignment given by the teacher.

The poetry chosen should reflect the state of mind of the adolescent. Authors of the twentieth century and the latter part of the nineteenth often reflect this state of mind. Theater can also be important. Even though it is difficult to find time to offer so much material in this grade, the presentation of a play can be very enriching for the students, especially when different levels of ability are found in the class.

Suggestions for Topics and Content for Spanish Lessons by Grades

Topics and Content	1	2	3	4	5	6	7	8	Specifications
Courtesy, phrases, greetings, goodbye	x	x	x	x	x	x	x	x	
Numbers: 1 – 50	x								
Numbers: 1 – 100		x							
Numbers: 1 – 1000			x	x	x	x	x	x	
Human body	x	x	x	x	x	x	x	x	
Colors	x	x	x	x	x	x	x	x	From 4th on can use hues
Clothing		x	x	x	x	x	x	x	
Musical instruments		x	x	x	x	x	x	x	
Animals	x	x	x	x					
Plants			x	x	x				
Food		x	x	x		x	x	x	
School	x	x	x	x	x	x	x	x	Beginning with classroom objects
The home and its parts			x	x	x	x	x	x	
The farm			x	x					
The garden			x	x	x				
The family		x	x	x	x	x	x	x	
Occupations and professions			x	x	x	x	x	x	
The seasons	x	x	x	x	x	x	x	x	
Months, weeks, days		x	x	x	x	x	x	x	
The date			x	x	x	x	x	x	
The clock, time			x	x	x	x	x	x	
Personal information	x	x	x	x	x	x	x	x	
Friends			x	x	x	x	x	x	
Likes and preferences		x	x	x	x	x	x	x	
Daily routines			x	x	x	x	x	x	
Sports			x	x	x	x	x	x	
Nature and the environment	x	x	x	x	x	x	x	x	
Means of transportation			x	x	x	x	x	x	
State geography				x	x				
Hispanic geography				x	x	x	x	x	Spain, Latin America, Caribbean
Spanish-speaking countries						x	x	x	
Folk dances	x	x	x	x	x	x			
History of Spain						x			Geography, ballads, El Cid, Rome
Pre-columbian cultures					x	x	x	x	
Teotihuacan					x	x	x	x	

FESTIVALS	1	2	3	4	5	6	7	8	
Christmas	x	x	x	x	x	x	x	x	
End of year				x	x	x	x	x	
Epiphany	x	x	x	x					
All Souls Day					x	x	x	x	
Halloween	x	x	x	x	x				
Thanksgiving		x	x	x	x	x	x	x	
May 5th				x	x	x	x	x	
September 16th						x	x	x	
Columbus Day				x	x	x	x		

Biographies	1	2	3	4	5	6	7	8	
Saints		X							
Painters						X	X	X	
Musicians						X	X	X	
Writers						X	X	X	
	1	**2**	**3**	**4**	**5**	**6**	**7**	**8**	
Poets						X	X	X	
Leaders							X	X	
Descriptions					X	X	X	X	
Physical: people, places, objects			X	X	X	X	X	X	
Climate, the weather			X	X	X	X	X	X	
Trips					X	X	X	X	
States of mind: a) personal				X	X	X	X	X	
b) the others					X	X	X	X	
Health				X	X	X	X	X	
Future plans						X	X	X	
Personal Relations					X	X	X	X	
Friendship					X	X	X	X	
Courtship							X	X	
Dating								X	
Writing letters					X	X	X	X	
Marriage								X	
Actions	X	X	X	X	X	X	X	X	
Proverbs					X	X	X	X	
Tongue-twisters				X	X	X	X	X	
Idiomatic expressions					X	X	X	X	

Suggestions of Means and Methods

little emphasis: X   emphasis: XX   great emphasis: XXX

	1	2	3	4	5	6	7	8
poetry and recitations	xxx	xxx	xxx	xxx	xxx	xxx	xxx	xxx
songs	xxx	xxx	xxx	xx	xx	xx	xx	xx
dances	xxx	xxx	xx	x	x	x	x	x
clapping games	xxx	xxx	xx					
finger games	xxx	xxx						
plays	xxx	xxx	xxx	xxx	xxx	xxx	xxx	xxx
skits (role playing)		xx	xxx	xxx	xxx	xxx	xxx	xxx
speech exercises				x	xx	xxx	xxx	xxx
tongue-twisters			xxx	xx	xx			
rhythmical gestures	xxx	xxx	xxx	xx	x	x	x	x
clapping and stamping	xxx	xxx	xx	xx	x	x	x	x
commands and orders	xxx	xxx	xxx	xxx	xxx	xxx	xxx	xxx
games with dialogues	xxx	xxx	xxx	xx	x	x	x	x
games movements	xxx	xxx	xxx	xx	x	x	x	x
hand painted illustrations	x	x	xxx	xxx	xxx	xxx	xxx	xxx
artistic printed illustrations			xxx	xxx	xxx	xxx	xxx	xxx
felt board	xxx	xxx	xx	x				
hand made puppets	xxx	xxx	xx	x				
hand made costumes and masks	xxx	xxx	xx					
descriptions	xx	xxx	xxx	xxx	xxx	xxx	xxx	xxx
picture dictations		x	xx	xxx	xxx	xxx	xxx	xxx
objects (non-plastic)	xxx	xxx	xxx	xx	xx	xx	xx	xx
dolls (hand made)	xxx	xxx	xx					
scenes from nature	xxx	xxx	xxx					
grains, fabrics, clay, etc.			xxx					
recapitulation of stories (oral)	xxx	xxx	xxx	xxx	xxx	xxx	xxx	xxx
children's stories (oral)	xxx	xxx	xxx	xx	x			
legends (oral)		xxx	xxx	xxx	xxx	xxx	xxx	xxx
legends (writing)				xx	xxx	xxx	xxx	xxx
prose (writing)				xx	xxx	xxx	xxx	xxx
biographies (writing)						xx	xx	xxx
grammatical rules (writing)				xx	xxx	xxx	xxx	xxx
readers				x	xxx	xxx	xxx	xxx
legends (reading)				xx	xxx	xxx	xxx	xxx
biographies							xxx	xxx
prose (reading)				xx	xxx	xxx	xxx	xxx
literary passages					x	xx	xx	xxx
reading and investigation					xx	xxx	xxx	xxx
conversations and dialogues	xxx	xxx	xxx	xxx	xxx	xxx	xxx	xxx
partner conversations					xx	xxx	xxx	xxx

Chapter 3

Learning the Language Grade by Grade

Thanks to play and imagination, the inert nature of adults—a chair, a book, any object suddenly acquires its own life. Through the magical virtue of language, of gesture, of symbol, or of action, the child creates a living world, in which objects are capable of responding to his questions. Language, stripped of its intellectual meanings, stops being a collection of signs and becomes a delicate organism of magical magnetization. There is no distance between the name and the thing, and to pronounce a word is to set in motion the reality that it designates. The representation is equivalent to a real reproduction of the object, just as for a primitive person, a sculpture is not a representation but a double of the object represented. Speaking becomes an activity that creates realities, that is, a poetic activity. The child, by virtue of magic, creates a world for his imagination and thus resolves his solitude. He becomes one with his environment. Conflict is reborn when the child stops believing in the power of words or of gestures.

– Octavio Paz
From his book ***The Labyrinth of Solitude and Other Works***

The First Stage: An Oral Approach for Grade 1 to 3

During the first three years of learning, the experience of the pupil is totally oral. Through gestures, mimicry, recitation of poems, rhymes, songs, games, and plays, the child little by little acquires a vocabulary. This is where the teacher must be clear about *what she is teaching*. It is important for the teacher to acquire a sense for the development and maturity of the class and the child, to present the material with a clear sequence and progression. The preparation has to be deep and orderly, and familiarization with the main curriculum is imperative. In the first stage the teacher is going to lay the grammatical foundations, and encourage the child's acquisition of vocabulary.

Narration

Stories are one of the tools used in language teaching. Stories re-create pictorially a narrative history, a fable, a legend, or a fairy tale, helping the child to connect intimately with the language. By means of gestures, original drawings, books with illustrations, or objects, it is possible to re-create the story. It is not necessary for the student to understand the meaning of every word; what is important is to capture the essence, to imagine the story through the sound and the melody of the language, and to enjoy the experience. The story is a good tool for developing and reinforcing a basic vocabulary, while new terms are being introduced.

As an example of one method, among many others, let us look at an activity for the first grade: *El Coquí Puertorriqueño.*

To present the story, the teacher creates a feeling that something wonderful is going to happen. He points out the big briefcase that he has brought (holding the materials he is going to work with) and then he asks for silence as he places all these wonderful things and begins . . .

Suddenly, a tiny toad appears and introduces himself:

Coquí: ¡Hola, buenos días, soy un coquí¡

Everybody: ¡Hola, buenos días, coquí¡

. . . and the coquí moves to where everyone can see him. Of course, this has all been planned, and the teacher now has the perfect place to carry out the story. The teacher says, "escuchen en silencio" and begins to tell the story, using a felt board or cardboard, illustrations, and objects that complement the illustrations, placing each element in its proper place, so that at the end of the tale there is a "picture" of the story.

He begins:

Había una vez un coquí	*Points to the toad.*
que vivía en una roca,	*Places a rock near the toad.*
en una roca debajo del mar.	*Places drawing of a rock and the sea on top of the rock.*
La roca	*Points again to the rock.*
soñaba y soñaba con despertar.	*Makes a gesture of sleeping and dreaming and waking up.*

El sol,	*Places drawing of the sun.*
con el viento	*Makes sound of wind and places.*
la tierra	*Piece of earth in shape of island.*
y las olas	*Makes wavy gesture with*
	hands and adds picture of waves.
habló.	*Speaking gesture with hand,*
	mouth.
Y todos juntos a la roca	*Points to class and to sleeping rock*
despertaron.	*that wakes up.*
El sol calentaba.	*From here on everything done*
	with gestures and sounds,
	pointing to figures.

el viento soplaba,

las olas bailaban

la tierra temblaba y la roca despertaba.

El coquí, agarradito a la roca, muy contento cantaba:
coquí, coquí, coquí, qui, qui, qui (twice)
Todos los niños (pointing to all) felices estaban y cantaban así:

(First the teacher sings the song, and of course in the chorus everyone will join in)

El coquí, el coquí a mí me encanta,

es tan dulce el cantar del coquí,

por las noches al ir a acostarme

me adormece cantándome así:

Chorus: coquí, coquí,, coquí, qui, qui, qui (repeat).

Now mark the rhythm snapping fingers (twice).

Now with palms clapping (twice).

Now whistling (twice).

And finishing with: COQUÍ.

Upon finishing the story the children have a picture of the story, they know the "coquí," and feel motivated to continue singing the song that delighted them. In class we repeat the story, like a short poem, with gestures, ending with the song of the "coquí,." Then two or three questions are asked, showing the "coquí," and inviting the students to answer chorally:

¿Qué es? Es un coquí.

¿Canta el coquí? Sí, canta el ccoquí.

¿Es pequeño el coquí? Sí, es pequeño.

The next class the activity is repeated and new questions are asked:

¿Está contento el coquí? Sí, está contento el coquí.

¿De qué color es el coquí? El coquí es marrón.

After several days working with the story, the song is incorporated as part of the routine at the end of the class, before the farewell.

The last step for this activity is the dramatization with costumes: a frog, the wind, the earth, the birth of the waves, a rock, and the sun. These elements are distributed among the students, and little by little, the story is acted out in this way.

Following is a fable about the lion and the mouse for second grade.

El león y el ratón
había una vez un ratón,
pequeño como un botón.
Cuando la luna asomaba,
él su comida buscaba.
Una noche un león lo siguió,
y de un zarpazo lo cogió.
"Por favor, déjame marchar,
algún día me has de necesitar."
El león en las redes cayó,
vino el ratón y lo salvó.

Each animal could be represented by a musical instrument: xylophone for the mouse, and güiro (gourd instrument) for the lion. While the class recites together, the teacher plays one or the other instrument. When the mouse speaks, only one pupil does the part:

> Había una vez un ratón (pentatonic xylophone)
> pequeño como un botón.
> Cuando la luna asomaba,
> él (xylophone) su comida buscaba.
> Una noche un león lo siguió (güiro like footsteps)
> y de un zarpazo (güiro) lo cogió.
> "Por favor, déjame marchar,
> algún día me has de necesitar." (pupil)
> El león en las redes cayó, (güiro like a blow)
> vino el ratón (xylophone) y lo salvó.

Once the students know it by heart, four of them dramatize it: a lion, a mouse, a moon, and the nets. The lion and the mouse have masks. One child holds up the paper moon, another a cloth as though it were the net that he will throw over the lion.

Another example is the story of Goldilocks and the Three Bears. It is a children's tale that they all know in third grade, and the teacher should present it as a challenge.

Teacher: "I know that you know the story, but I want to see if you can tell it to me in Spanish." Then the teacher can tell the story using a book, little by little showing the illustrations. Upon finishing, the new vocabulary should be emphasized: taza, caliente, frío, templado, blando, dura, escalera, etc. Then she asks, "¿Es la taza de osito niño?" "¿Es la taza pequeña o grande?" using the illustrations and objects necessary for presenting the new vocabulary. From that moment, the student should answer with complete sentences. For example: "Sí, es la taza de osito niño."

In the next class, the teacher can bring a felt board with cutouts to illustrate the story. Then she will call on a volunteer to narrate the first scene. The volunteer presents, with the cutouts, the bears, the house, and a table with three cups of different sizes: a big one, a medium one, and a little one. Another student will come forth to recapitulate the sizes of the chairs and beds. Another one tells how Goldilocks drinks from the cups, sits in the chairs, and lies down in the beds. And another one will end the story with the arrival and the surprise of the bears. The cutouts can move and walk around the felt board. Meanwhile the teacher is orchestrating the movements.

And in the following class, the children summarize the story as the teacher shows the illustrations and cutouts, saying, for example: "hay tres osos, papá oso, mamá oso y el osito niño . . . ."

Vocabulary as a Means of Expression and its Development in the Class

In the early grades, speech has greater importance because of the formative powers of the language. The teacher has to be extremely careful in the correct pronunciation, intonation, and vocalization of the language. During the first three years of language learning, the child should acquire it as he acquires a habit, and as he acquires the native tongue. The child has relationships with the sounds more than with the meanings, so that he "lives" the language, in his imagination, instinctively.

For Rudolf Steiner, language is the expression of the world of feelings, and it unites us with the objects of the world around us. When we combine a vowel with a consonant, we are combining sympathy and antipathy. Vowels, as expressions of the soul, contain feeling; consonants, as imitations of external things, have the function of expressing antipathy, through the dental, guttural, nasal, lip, and tongue sounds. In the "A" (ah) lies an expression of wonder; in the "E" (eh) that of resistance; in the "I" (ee) that of the feeling for oneself; in the "U" (oo) that of fear or awe. Language is born from the relation of the human being with the cosmos, and as a consequence of this relation, sounds arise. This is why Steiner advises us to be very conscious of the power of language and its articulation. Another example he uses is that of the variation in meaning of the words used for naming the head:

> **Kopf**: describes the form.
> **Testa**: describes the function.
> **Head**: describes the position.

The different words in languages are taken from different connections . . .language is intimately connected to feeling, Steiner explains.

The feeling of wonder unites us with the world around us, and this is why we develop language. Objects reveal themselves in the form of pictures, and we simply cultivate a relation with them that stimulates language, which has to do with the organization of the ego. In the ego lives the unique quality of language, as a living and creative force. Sensitivity to the beauty of language, which develops between the ages of seven and fourteen, helps in forming the ego and a social conscience.

In the following pages we offer some examples of activities for working with the language in its totality, in a natural, unconscious manner, integrating specific aspects of the language, and laying grammatical foundations.

First Grade

Example 1

Poem: Sale el sol

> Sale el sol por la mañana,
> sale el sol a calentar,
> siempre sale por el este,
> yo lo voy a saludar,
> ¿cómo estás? astro de fuego
> ¿cómo estás? amigo sol,
> alumbrando noche y día,
> dándoles luz y calor.
>
> Song: Hola, hola
> Hola, hola, ¿cómo estás?
> Buenos días, vengo a saludar.
> Yo estoy bien, y tú, ¿qué tal?
> Muy contento de estar todos aquí.

The student repeats until he has memorized each word, the intonation, musicality, action, and movement of the poem and the song, without having to know the meaning of each of the words. The child creates an image inwardly by means of gestures, mimicking, intonation, and the mood that the teacher reveals when presenting them. The basic vocabulary that is built up can include some of the incidental words from the poem or song, and also the vocabulary of courtesy, greetings, and goodbye. These words can be practiced by means of an action intended to provoke a response. For example, using the poem and the song as starting points, one could create a list of words and expressions that we think they should learn:

> Hola, buenos días.
> ¿Cómo estás?
> Bien gracias.
> ¿Y usted / tú?
> ¿Cómo te llamas?
> Me llamo . . .
> Mucho gusto.
> Con permiso.
> Por favor.

Hasta luego.
Adiós.
Gracias.
Later we set up activities related to the theme.

Example 2: A Puppet

A puppet visits the class and wants to meet the children and learn their names.

The teacher says, "Hoy contamos con la visita de Lola, ella quiere conocerlos y aprender sus nombres." (She gets Lola.)

Teacher:	"Esta es Lola."
Lola:	"Hola."
All repeat:	"Hola, Lola."
Lola:	"Buenos días."
All repeat:	"Buenos días, Lola."

(By now the children understand that the puppet is Lola.)

The teacher says: "Escuchen." (makes gesture of listening and puts a finger on her mouth.)

Teacher: (singing) "Yo me llamo . . .¿cómo te llamas tú?"

Lola: (hablando) "Yo me llamo Lola."

Teacher: "Mucho gusto, Lola."

Lola: "Mucho gusto." (they shake hands while saying "mucho gusto.")

Teacher: "Vamos a conocer a todos estos niños." (making a gesture toward the children.)

Lola: "Sí" (Lola begins to walk toward the children, toward their desks. The teacher marks her steps with a sound: ta, tac, ta, tac . . . . The sound of Lola's steps helps keep a certain anticipation, which creates silence, and avoids any interruption. Lola also indicates that one must be quiet, as the teacher did.) (Reaching a child.)

Lola: "Yo me llamo Lola, ¿cómo te llamas tú?" (If the child doesn't answer, the teacher helps him. Usually they will answer only with their name, in which case the teacher says, "Yo me llamo . . ." and repeats the name of the child.)

Lola: "Mucho gusto . . . . "
Child: "Mucho gusto, Lola." (if not, the teacher helps him)
Lola: "Adiós."
Child: "Adiós."
And Lola goes on to the next child.

In this way, by visiting and stimulating responses in all the pupils, most of them will have "recorded" part of the basic vocabulary.

Example 3

Lola presents: "Por las montañas, valles y lagos,
                    camina, camina mi Lola
                    y a todo el que encuentre,
                    lo saluda con un ¡Hola!"
The children repeat: "Hola, Lola."
Lola reviews: "Me llamo," "mucho gusto," "hasta luego," but this time with only three or four children.

The next day Lola presents, ¿cómo estás? . . .bien, gracias, ¿y usted / tú?" At first they all repeat chorally, then Lola visits three or four children. In the following days Lola reviews everything: Me llamo, mucho gusto, y ¿cómo estás?

To practice this vocabulary, each time different "characters" visit the class, the same list of selected terms are to be used. Also, in the daily interaction inside and outside the classroom, these elements of greeting, courtesy, and goodbye are going to be reinforced in a more casual way.

Each theme that we present should be carefully studied. For example, colors:

Which colors will I work on in first, second, and third grades? What activity will I design for this purpose? How should I incorporate this theme with others? How should I practice it? In what way will I go about sowing and harvesting everything, little by little, expanding, adding new elements, relating some things with others, until we reach a point where the child may begin to use the language to express himself and communicate?

The following is an example of how to integrate another theme:

Lola should have a rest, so that the children don't lose interest. She brings a friend to class: Nina, the butterfly. Nina will present the theme of colors and will carry out a review of the vocabulary presented previously.

Example 4

Lola arrives at class and greets:

	"Hola, buenos días."
All repeat:	"Hola, buenos días."
Lola:	"¿Cómo están? (Here some children will repeat the question and others will answer it.)
Lola:	"Esta es Nina." (Some children will repeat.)
Lola:	"Hola, Nina."
All respond:	"Hola, Nina."
Teacher:	"Lola se tiene que ir, digámosle . . .adiós Lola."
All say:	"Adiós, Lola."

The teacher takes Lola to her "house" and comes back singing with Nina:

"Una mariposa que vuela por el aire
busca un amigo, ¿dónde irá a parar?"

Nina goes flying about as she sings, and stops on the shoulder, the table, or the head of a child. Nina carries out the same previous dialogue of Lola: *Hola, me llamo . . .mucho gusto . . ., ¿cómo estás? . . .bien, gracias . . . ¿Y usted / tú? . . . hasta luego . . . adiós.* In this manner she visits three or four children and sings her song each time that she flies.

The next class Nina arrives alone. She greets, asks everyone how they are and introduces her friends who are butterflies of different colors in a basket (these can be of cardboard, felt, or paper).

Nina says to all:	"Hola, buenos días."
All repeat:	"Hola, buenos días."
Nina:	"¿Cómo están?"
All respond:	"Bien, gracias, ¿y usted / tú?"
Nina:	"Bien, gracias."
Nina:	"Hoy están conmigo varias mariposas de distintos colores que deseo presentarles." (Nina goes to the basket and takes out a butterfly.)
Nina:	"Este es el color AMARILLO."
All repeat:	"Este es el color AMARILLO."
Nina:	"¿De qué color es?"
All respond:	"Es amarillo."

It is best to present only three or four colors, and in subsequent classes add one or two, ending with the seven colors of the rainbow: yellow, red, blue, orange, green, violet, and indigo.

It is also advisable to present the colors in lessons of three periods:
Period 1: name the color, repeat it.
Period two: point out the color that the teacher names.
Period three: identify the color by its name.

Example 5

After presenting three or four colors, they can be reviewed in the following way:

The teacher says, "¿Quién puede señalar el color amarillo?" (The teacher makes a gesture of pointing out, the children raise their hands, the teacher chooses one, the child goes to the front, points out the color and repeats its name. We all thank him and continue with others.)

In the next class the colors are reviewed and then we go on to identification. The teacher asks, "¿Qué color es?"

The child identifies the color by its name, "Es el color amarillo."

After the students have mastered the colors, we can go through the next activity:

Nina arrives, gives a greeting, asks how they are . . .

Nina: "Hoy vamos a jugar un juego. Yo voy
a preguntar, tú vas a contestar."
Nina takes out the first butterfly:
"¿Qué color es?"

A child answers, and if the answer is correct, she goes to the front and takes the butterfly with the identified color. All the colors are reviewed with this question. If there is one that is not identified, the color is repeated chorally, and the butterfly is left in the basket. After all have been identified, and the children chosen are at the front, Nina will guide the activity.

Nina indicates to the children in the front to follow her. Then she begins to sing with pauses so the children can repeat the song:

"Unas mariposas, vuelan por el aire, dan una vuelta y se pararán."
(They imitate.)
Nina: "mariposa color amarillo."
Yellow butterfly: "aquí" (The teacher should guide the child.)
Nina says: "mariposa color amarillo vuela a la canasta".
(The butterfly flies to the basket, and we dismiss the child with thanks. Now we can count the remaining butterflies:)
"A ver, a ver, ¿cuántas mariposas quedan?" uno, dos . . .

Thus we continue again with the song until all the butterflies have been put away and then Nina says goodbye.

Second Grade

As in the first grade, in the second and third grades sense impressions are received through nature. Class activities should also be taken from the world around us.

Example 1: Recitation, the Human Body

Niño, niña, vamos a jugar
yo te voy a preguntar,
tú me vas a contestar.
Los ojos ¿para qué son?
Los ojos son para ver.
La nariz ¿para qué es?
La nariz es para oler.

>La boca ¿para qué es?
>La boca es para hablar y para comer.
>Las orejas ¿para qué son?
>Las orejas son para escuchar.
>Los dedos ¿para qué son?
>Los dedos son para tocar.
>Y el corazón ¿para qué es?
>El corazón es para amar.

In second grade we also have a very good opportunity to introduce the qualities of adverbs and adjectives through fables.

Example 2: Fable of the Hare and the Tortoise.

After telling the story to the class with visual aids, the teacher asks the students to identify and name in Spanish the animal protagonists and the elements of the landscape of the fable. Then questions such as these can be asked:

¿Es la tortuga rápida ø lenta? La tortuga es lenta.
¿Cómo iba la liebre, lentamente o rápidamente? La liebre iba rápidamente.

Example 3

By means of drawings of animals the teacher can start the following game (15 or more animals are needed).

1. Estoy pensando en un animal, es mediano, no es muy inteligente y vuela. ¿Qué animal es? (un pato)
2. Estoy pensando en un animal, es pequeño, tiene antenas y trabaja mucho. Qué animal es? (una hormiga)

3. Estoy pensando en un animal, es mediano, es muy rápido, salta por el campo y come zanahorias. ¿Qué animal es? (un conejo)

The ideal is to create bigger challenges and expose the students to many nouns, adjectives, verbs, adverbs, articles, and prepositions. Thus, basic elements of grammar and vocabulary are learned in a natural way.

Third Grade

In third grade we introduce the qualities (adjectives) of things (nouns) in a pictorial way.

Example 1

El elefante es grande.
El ratón es pequeño.
El león es fuerte.
La zorra es inteligente.
La serpiente es larga.
El mono es simpático.

It is also possible to present the relationship between noun and adjective by way of a game of antonyms, using drawings.

Example 2

La casa es nueva / la casa es vieja.
El niño está sucio / el niño está limpio.
El helado está frío / el café está caliente.
El dibujo es feo / el dibujo es lindo.
El pantalón es largo / el pantalón es corto.

After this exercise we invite the students to form sentences that refer to objects of the classroom. Rhythmically, with movements and/or a song, the adverbs of location can be presented:

Izquierda, izquierda, (teacher raises right hand facing them)
derecha, derecha,
delante, detrás,
uno, dos y tres (clapping.)

Izquierda, derecha, delante, detrás,
encima, abajo, delante, detrás,
dentro, fuera y arriba.

Then, during the second phase of the class questions like the following can be asked:

¿Dónde está la pizarra? La pizarra está delante.
¿Dónde está la puerta? La puerta está a la izquierda.
¿Dónde están sus cuadernos? Los cuadernos están encima de la mesa.

Already in first and second grade the students have been exposed to the relation of noun/verb through the animals and their actions; now, in third grade, this relation is transferred from the external (the animal world) to the inner (the individual, oneself).

Example 3

Yo salto, yo camino.
Yo paro a descansar.
Yo como, yo bebo.
Yo canto sin parar.
Yo hablo, yo escucho.
Yo estudio en mi hogar.
Yo abro, yo miro.
Yo corro a la mar.
Yo leo, yo escribo
y me siento en mi lugar.

An important part of the teaching of Spanish is the learning of the personal pronouns. In Spanish they are numerous, and it requires less effort if the teacher begins teaching them at an early age. It can begin with a game as early as the first grade.

Example 4:Yo, Tú

All:	¿Quién tomó la galleta del galletero?
Teacher:	María tomó la galleta del galletero.
María:	¿Quién, yo?
All:	Sí, tú.
María:	Yo no fui.
Todos:	¿Quién, pues?
María:	Bill.
All:	Bill tomó la galleta del galletero . . .

(The game continues as another child is named, while the rhythm is kept by clapping.)
In third grade the third person singular is introduced.

Example 5: Él, Ella y Usted.

Teacher:	¿Qué instrumento tocas tú?
John:	Yo toco el piano.
All:	Juan toca el piano, él toca el piano.

This example is repeated several times, and then other objects are used such as pencils, paintbrushes, books, etc., which can be distributed among the students.

Example 6

Teacher:	¿Escribes tú con el lápiz?
Girl:	Sí, yo escribo con el lápiz.
Teacher:	¿Con qué escribe ella?
All:	Ella escribe con el lápiz.

The material that the children memorize in the first three grades, repeated chorally or individually, is of great usefulness in the later grades where we bring to a conscious level all these elements of grammar:

- The relation of the noun with action,
- The relation of the noun with adjectives and articles that agree in gender and number,
- The difference in number and gender of the noun,
- Personal pronouns in the singular, prepositions, conjugations, adverbs, interrogatives, and simple sentences.

The Second Stage: Integrating Writing, Reading, and Grammar

Introduction

After these three completely oral years, we move on to writing, reading, and the teaching of grammar. Obviously the oral phase never ends. That is why from fourth grade on we begin to expand the oral experience by joining it to writing and reading. Likewise, we begin to make grammar rules of the language conscious, as many of them were acquired unconsciously in previous years, like acquiring a habit.

Narration and Re-telling

In the oral sphere, Waldorf education emphasizes the importance of re-telling, whether it be personal experiences, short stories, legends, anecdotes, or histories. Re-telling requires memory as well as imagination, a place where feelings are alive. Moreover, re-living a story opens a path to the written form, material that can then be read by one or by others.

For fourth, fifth, and sixth grades, brief stories are recommended, told and re-told by the teacher. She may add elements to the narrative, which is repeated with gestures and adequate intonation according to the tone indicated by the story. Drawings, illustrations, and a list of key words may be used to facilitate understanding of the story. Later it is necessary to elaborate in more detail, and then one can repeat the key vocabulary and idiomatic expressions. Now the students are ready to tell it themselves. This re-telling can be in their language; using this procedure, the teacher can corroborate their comprehension. If the student re-tells the story in the foreign language, it is advisable for the teacher to copy it on the board, guiding the process, condensing and/or summarizing. The re-telling can also be done by way of questions that the teacher formulates. Finally, the student can copy the story in his Spanish notebook. This material can be used later for reading, for a grammar lesson, or for a dramatic representation, depending on the material used.

In seventh and eighth grades, re-telling acquires greater importance, forming an essential part of the lesson, together with writing and reading in the language. An unlimited number of topics can be worked on using the story and the re-telling, not only for developing a required topic, but also for practicing the language already acquired. Personal experiences can be used for this type of re-telling.

Writing and Reading

Steiner explains that narrative descriptions of what the children have seen and heard, and the telling of real experiences should be the major source of inspiration for written work.

Writing and reading emerge gradually out of painting and drawing. Step by step the form of writing arises out of the form of drawings, and from there one goes on to reading. It is highly important to understand the reasons for this sequence. In one sense writing is more alive than reading. In writing we have continued imitating universal forms, if we allow the letters to arise out of drawing. The printed letter, on the other hand, is something extraordinarily abstract at the beginning of the reading process. This is why Steiner states that, out of drawing, which has developed out of painting, the children should be guided by the inventiveness of the teacher, so that an artistic base is established for conventional writing.

If we go directly to reading, without respecting the sequence of speaking—writing— reading, we will find that we are upsetting and impeding progress in the language. If we read something that has no relation to the student, we are working in a vacuum, wasting precious time for the students and ourselves. What is important is that the student should understand first what he hears, answers, expresses, and only then should write it. Later, once this process has been carried out, the child is prepared to read the content of what he has heard.

The process of writing material that has been previously internalized allows the children to recognize what they are copying, and provides an initial feeling of confidence in writing and reading in the foreign language. Since they are familiarized with the sound and general content of the written material, they can begin to read orally with relatively few problems.

Grammar

As for grammar, Steiner tells us that this actually resides in our organism, and when we study it, we bring it to the consciousness. It is not until the age of nine or ten years that we change the unconscious element of the language of the early learning years, and take it to a conscious level in a rational way, presenting the grammar and the logic of the language. Dealing with language in connection with grammar is related to the development of the ego. It is not a question of how to develop the ego through grammar, but rather that simply bringing grammar to consciousness helps in the ego's development.

Our goal is not to teach grammar in a dry, pedantic way, but to bring awareness, in a natural and creative way, of the descriptive science of language. This would include the forms, functions, and sounds of words, as well as their interconnections and order in sentences. Such a study should likewise be a stimulus for correct writing.

To carry out this task of teaching grammar, we should understand Steiner's statements concerning the relation of the human being with noun, adjective, and verb, and how the development of our consciousness occurs in our relation with things, when we refer to them.

Steiner emphasizes the importance of knowing how significant it is for the human being to become conscious of the structure of language. "Only when the child learns to differentiate himself from the environment can he begin to examine what is in his speech." (***Rudolf Steiner's Curriculum for Waldorf School*** by Karl Stockmeyer).

For this reason we begin the teaching of grammar in fourth grade. The child is now prepared to take up that unconscious element of language learning, and can begin to become conscious of Spanish grammar.

Next is a table detailing the suggested grammatical elements for the fourth through eighth grades.

Suggested Diagram for Teaching Grammar from Fourth through Eighth Grades

Elements	When	What
	4th grade	Gender, number, agreement of adjectives with articles.
1. Nouns	5th grade	Formation of plural; non-plural nouns. Change of gender in some nouns.
	6th grade	Application of learned materials.
	7th and 8th	Abstract and concrete nouns.
2. Adjectives	4th grade	Descriptives: agreement with nouns, gender and number. Neuters.
	4th to 8th	Possesives
	4th to 8th	Quantity, indefinites.
	5th	Use of "de" as a possessive.
	5th to 8th	Shortening of some adjectives and comparatives.
	6th to 8th	Demonstratives.
3. Articles	4th to 8th	Definite and indefinite. Gender and number.

4. Prepositions	4th grade	Most common: en, entre, de, a, con, para.
	5th grade	Sin, por, desde, hasta, durante.
	6th to 8th	Use of "por" y "para" "a" personal.
5. Conjunctions	4th grade	Most common: y, ni, pero, porque.
	5th to 8th	Mientras, o / u, si, como, pues, que, aunque.
	7th and 8th	Use of "que" and its omission in English when use as a conjuction.
6. Interjections	4th to 8th	Emphatic use: admiration, exclamation and beginning and end puctuation.
7. Adverbs	4th grade	*Of time*: ayer, ahora, hoy, mañana, todavía, después, luego, siempre, nunca, más tarde, pronto. *Of place*: aquí, allí, allá, ahí *Of degree*: poco, mucho, muy, igual. *Of manner*: lento, rápido, bien, mal, así.
	5th grade	Previous plus: entonces, jamás, ya, fuera, afuera, atrás, detrás, al frente, adelante, dentro, debajo, encima, etc.

	6th to 8th	Use and application.
8. Pronouns	4th grade	Personals.
	5th and 6th	Personals and the ommission of "it"
	7th grade	Direct object.
	8th grade	Indirect object.

9. Verbs

Clasification

Regulars	4th to 8th
Irregulars	4th to 8th
Reflexives	4th to 8th
Reciprocals	7th and 8th
Unipersonals	4th to 8th

Voice

Active	4th to 8th
Passive	8th grade

Moods

Indicative	4th to 8th
Imperative	4th to 8th
Infinitive	4th to 8th
Progressive	7th and 8th
Potential or conditional	8th grade

Tenses

Present of indicative	4th to 8th	
Past of indicative (imperfect and simple past)	7th and 8th	
Future of indicative (perfect)	8th grade	
A. *Indicative*: present	4th grade	Regulars: -ar Irregulars: ser, estar, tener, jugar.
	5th grade	Regulars: -ar, -er, -ir

	5th grade	Irregulars and reflexives.
	6th grade	Irregulars.
Past	7th grade	Irregulars; simple past.
		Imperfect; reflexives.
Future	8th grade	Irregulars; perfect.
B. Infinitive	4th grade	Regulars.
	5th grade	Infinitives + prepositions a, para, por.
	6th to 8th	Infinitives with two verbs.
C. Progressive	8th grade	Formation of gerund and participle with presente, past and future of estar in the indicative.
D. Potential or conditional	7th and 8th	Commands and favors.
E. Imperative	4th to 8th	

Fourth Grade

In the fourth grade the class begins to create their own books, first copying what they have learned in previous years, and then what they are learning in the current year. It is thus possible to observe the importance of each stage. Early in the fourth grade the student works hard to honor the language in its external form, which is writing. This process helps him to reinforce spelling, the use of old and new vocabulary. Besides, he has in his hands reading material with which we can work on pronunciation and grammar.

We begin the year with a review and practice of all the basic vocabulary of previous years, using actions and situations that we create to stimulate student responses. This gives us the opportunity of evaluating how much has been retained, what needs reinforcing and expanding. At the same time, a space is opened up so the new students can become integrated into the class. This is the right moment to begin the preparation of the book or notebook. Before turning it in, the student will design the cover and will write "español," the grade, and his or her name on it, and will draw a small, simple picture for identification.

The first page can stay blank, since as soon as the student has memorized the poem recited at the opening of class fairly well, he can copy it there. Another alternative is to begin the lesson with the writing of a poem learned in previous years. When the class has finished copying, it reads chorally what has been copied. Later it can be read by rows, and finally, individually. When the reading has finished, it can be illustrated in the notebook.

From there one can go on to oral review. This begins with personal information in the form of a dialogue:

¿Cómo te llamas? ¿cómo estás? ¿dónde vives? ¿cuántos años tienes?, ¿cuándo es tu cumpleaños? ¿qué te gusta? ¿dónde naciste? etc.

One way to present this work is by giving information about the teacher first:

"Hola, me llamo Sr./Sra./Srta._____¿y tú?"
"Tengo_____años, ¿y tú?"

In this way the student refreshes his memory and the new ones can repeat and begin to understand.

The second part of the review, just like the first, is through questions:
"¿Cómo te llamas? ¿Dónde vives? . . ."
The answers should be complete, emphasizing the correct forming of sentences. And the third part of the review is the copying of that information in their grammar notebooks:

Me llamo_____
Vivo en _____
Tengo _____años.

They have to complete the blank spaces, and then copy the questions that correspond to the previous information.

Through writing the teacher tries to bring awareness to the students of the different sounds and their representation in spelling. It is recommended that phonetics be worked on by the teacher's speaking, and not through pronunciation and spelling rules. On the basis of the teacher's pronunciation, the students gradually grasp the different phonetic sounds, which later are noticed again in writing and reading.

Below we offer a staggered example of the review at the beginning of each year, which increases in complexity and reinforces and introduces elementary grammatical notions.

Parts of the Body

In previous years the student may have learned the poem on the parts of the body (example 1, second grade, first phase). This can be used as an introduction and as a reading.

a. Oral

1. First the part of the body being presented is named and pointed to,

2. The child is asked to point to the part of the body the teacher indicates,

3. The child is asked to identify orally the part of the body that the teacher points to.

b. Writing and Drawing

On the board the following questions are presented: ¿Qué es? y ¿qué son?, together with drawings of different parts of the body which the students should copy and draw (here the verb "ser" can be introduced or reviewed).

c. Writing

The question is written on the board: ¿Qué hago con . . .? Los ojos, las manos, la nariz, los dedos, la boca, las piernas, la lengua, los pies, los brazos . . .

The actions are then determined orally and written on the board:

—Con los ojos: mirar, ver

—Con la nariz: oler . . .

—(Here infinitives of verbs are introduced or reviewed).

d. Oral and Written Questions

> —¿Cómo es mi nariz?
>
> —¿Cómo son mis manos?
>
> —(Here adjectives, possessive pronouns, gender and num
> ber can be worked on.)

e. Introduction of New Vocabulary on the Body, and the Process Begins again from (a)

Within this framework one should also review clothing, the year, the seasons, the months, the weather, the days of the week, numbers from 1 to 1000, clock time, daily routines, sports practiced by the students, pets, the family, tastes in food, and other topics. These reviews can be supported with rhymes, verses, and songs.

It is a good idea from fourth grade on to stimulate communication in Spanish with the teacher. One can gradually present a list of daily phrases for the students to use in different moments, such as: "no es justo," "puedo ir afuera?" "¿puedo ir al baño?," "no entiendo," and any other phrase that is considered appropriate. It is necessary to create a rhythm and a need so that these phrases can be used frequently and naturally.

The focus of fourth grade grammar is personal pronouns and regular verb conjugations in the present tense. Choral exercises with rhythmic movements are created for this purpose. Michael Navascués, in his article "*Waldorf Schools: Seventy-Six Years of Early Language Learning,*" states that "verb conjugations are learned by oral recitation, often accompanied by rhythmic movements, such as clapping hands with a neighbor or marching."

However, although they may repeat the conjugations chorally, this does not mean that they have learned them. From this point on, this area will be an arduous task for the Spanish teacher, since English does not express the same individuality in verb morphology, and there are fewer personal pronouns.

If in third grade practice with musical instruments (example 6, third grade) has been carried out, the student will be familiar with the topic; otherwise, this is the time to present this exercise. The exercise has the purpose of beginning to provide keys for conjugating the present tense of verbs ending in -ar. It is important to guide the student toward the discovery of the rule.

Example 1: Game / Dialogue
Topic: Verb Conjugation and Pronouns
Step 1:

Choose two boys and two girls to form two groups, and begin the following game-dialogue.

Teacher: ¿Qué instrumento tocas tú?
Boy: Yo toco el violín.
Teacher (to the class):
                  ¿Qué instrumento toca él?
All: El toca el violín.
Teacher (to a girl):
                  ¿Qué instrumento tocas tú?
Girl: Yo toco la guitarra.
Teacher (to the class):
                  ¿Qué instrumento toca ella?
All: Ella toca la guitarra.
(The exercise is repeated with two more pairs separated by sex.)

Teacher (pointing to the girls):
                  ¿Qué instrumento tocan ellas?
All: Ellas tocan la guitarra.
Teacher: ¿Qué instrumento tocan ellos?
All: Ellos tocan el violín.
Class asks the four children:
                  ¿Qué instrumento tocan ustedes?
Girls: Nosotras tocamos la guitarra.
Boys: Nosotros tocamos el violín.

Step 2

After they are all seated again.
Teacher: ¿Cuál es la acción principal de este juego?
Children: Tocar el violín, tocar la guitarra.
Teacher (to the class):
                  Repitamos todos juntos:

Yo toco, **tú** tocas, **él** toca, **ella** toca el violín y la guitarra,
Nosotros tocamos, **nosotras** tocamos, **ellos** tocan, **ellas** tocan el violín y la guitarra.
        (To be repeated three times.)

At this point in the exercise the teacher has two alternatives:
a) stop at this stage and create other similar activities with other regular verbs, or

b) continue toward awareness of the rules for the formation of the present tense of verbs ending in "ar."

When we continue with option (b), we should keep in mind the following recommendations:

One must deduce the grammar from prose selections, and deduce the rules from sentences, and then forget the sentences and remember the rules. A passage may be read, and the class will be encouraged to identify a particular concept, such as a verb. Then the teacher writes the rule concisely on the blackboard and the child should write it in his notebook.

Example 2
A. By Means of Sentences

1. Several sentences are put on the blackboard, showing changes in the verb depending on the person doing the action. (The same verb or another can be used; the teacher copies the sentences on the board).

Yo toco el violín y tú tocas la guitarra.
Ella toca el violín y él toca la guitarra.
Ellos tocan muy bien.
Nosotros tocamos el violín y la guitarra en la escuela.
(The students do not copy the examples.)

2. The sentences are read (select different students).

3. The teacher asks:
        ¿Cuál es la acción principal en las oraciones?
We go to the first sentence:
        ¿Quién toca el violín? (The answer is underlined.)
        ¿Quién toca la guitarra? (The answer is underlined.)
(Repeat with each example.)

4. We ask what difference can be observed in this action depending on the person who is doing it. (Here it will be necessary to guide them toward the correct answer.)

5. We go to the main action: TOCAR
    a. What part do the main action and the other forms have in common?
       TOC (the teacher can say that this part is called "raíz" or stem).
    b. What does the main action end in? "–AR"

Now we go on to copy, in order, the actions. "TOCAR"
The student says:

> Yo toco, tú tocas, él toca, ella toca, nosotros-nosotras
> tocamos, ellos-ellas tocan.

c. What tense is the action in?

> Present: hoy
> Past: ayer
> Future: mañana

d. Let's point out the endings according to the person who is doing the action:

> Yo . . . . o
> Tú . . . . .as
> Èl, ella . . . . a
> Nosotros, nosotras. . . . . amos
> Ellos, ellas. . . . . an

e. Therefore to form the present tense of an action verb ending in "ar," what do we have to do?

The student formulates the rule and the teacher writes it on the blackboard:

Example: "In Spanish to form the present tense of the regular verbs ending in "AR," we add to the stem the following endings: -o, -as, -a, -amos, -an.

The examples are erased from the board and the student writes the rule in his booklet.

One should have a booklet or part of the Spanish notebook designated for grammar. Steiner understands that memorization of grammatical rules corresponds to the development of the ego between the age of nine and twelve, and rules are taught via feeling, not intellect, and thus they can be memorized better. Writing the rule in the notebook helps memorization.

Students love to conjugate and to practice exercises:

Example (Oral)

Teacher:	Elena, ¿qué te gusta más? ¿pintar, cocinar o saltar?
Elena:	Me gusta pintar y cocinar.
Teacher:	Conjuga con Yo.
Elena:	Yo pinto y yo cocino.
All:	Ella pinta, ella cocina.
Teacher:	¿Dónde pintas tú?
Student:	Yo pinto en la escuela.

Steiner was asked the following question: Should we use the native language in the grammar lessons? He replied, "Proceed according to your convictions." (June 22, 1922)

B. Through a reading

"María de las Estrellas canta todas las mañanas mientras se prepara para ir a la escuela. Las canciones que ella canta son muy alegres. María canta muy bien. A Juan, su hermano, le gusta mucho como María canta. Yo canto cuando estoy contenta. Tengo dos amigos que cantan todo el tiempo y cuando estoy con ellos todos cantamos juntos. Yo canto muy mal, pero ellos cantan muy bien. ¿Cantas tú?"

A re-telling of the reading is carried out, and then we follow the same process that was used with sentences. With this reading we can also focus the student's awareness of the role played by the different parts of the sentence—the verb, the noun, the personal pronoun, the prepositions, and the adverbs. Simple exercises focusing on a part of the sentence can be done using, for instance, the interrogatives: ¿cómo?, ¿cuándo?, ¿dónde? y ¿qué ?

Begin with a simple phrase: (María canta) and with questions:

What action do we have here? Cantar.

Who does the action? María

How does María sing? We don't know, the sentence doesn't say. Let's describe the action: María canta muy bien.

What does María sing? It doesn't say, let's point out what María sings:

María canta muy bien una canción.

What type of song does María sing? It doesn't say, but we can describe the song:

María canta muy bien una canción alegre.

Which María? It doesn't say, but let's indicate which María is referred to:

María, la hermana de Juan, canta muy bien una canción alegre.

When does María sing? . . .

In this way the different parts of the sentence are presented, indicating what part it is, a conjugation, an adverb . . . .

By now the students have studied the parts of the sentence in the main lesson grammar, and often they will know the part of speech by its name. Later, in the higher grades the parts can be named directly. In fourth grade students recognize them as words that indicate action, which indicate names, which describe, etc.

One can do the same thing with other reading passages to focus on a particular part to be studied, or do other exercises with classroom objects, or by using sentences. Here are some examples:

The prepositions: "en," "de," "desde," "entre," "con." They define location, among other relationships, and in this sense they have a moral significance with reference to space and time.
Example:

Juan está sentado **en** el salón de arte.

Èl está sentado **entre** Julia y Manuel.

Si contamos los pasos **desde** la puerta **hasta** donde está Juan, sabemos que hay 20 pasos (We make bold what we want to focus on).

The steps to follow are:
1. Reading the sentences.
2. Ask questions on comprehension and new vocabulary:
¿Dónde está Juan? ¿Dónde está Juan sentado? . . .
3. Go to the underlined part:
¿Qué nos indica: en, de, entre, desde, hasta?

Here the child connects relationship, the use, and meaning of the preposition used in Spanish with the preposition in his own language. Later a practice sheet can be used.

The conjunctions "y," "ni," "pero," "que," "porque" are presented as pieces that join things (joining words).

Example 1: A Julio le gusta la música. A Julio le gusta bailar.

How can we join these two sentences and form a single one?

A Julio le gusta la música **y** le gusta bailar.

We can make an even shorter one:

A Julio le gusta la música **y** bailar.

Example 2: No me gustan las espinacas. No me gustan los berros.

No me gustan las espinacas ni los berros.

Example 3: Quiero ir al cine. Me gusta la película que muestran.

Quiero ir al cine **porque** me gusta la película que muestran.

Adverbs can be presented in a reading passage:

"Hoy es la gran carrera nacional de los cien metros. Crystal va a participar. Ella está en la salida, lista. Está muy nerviosa. Ella sabe que está bien preparada para la carrera. Dan la señal y Crystal sale rápidamente, toma la primera posición, sigue muy rápido. Todos la animan. Crystal gana la carrera."

Then it is read, re-told, and the new vocabulary is worked on. The teacher explains that there are key words that give us more information about what is happening, and she gives an example.

Let's look at the first sentence:

What does it tell us? That today is the national one hundred meter race. But there are two key words that tell us exactly when and which national race. (We continue in this way for the rest of the paragraph.)

Here are other examples:

Pedro llega bien. How does Pedro arrive? "bien"—this word helps the action.

Juan es mi mejor amigo. Who is Juan? "mi mejor amigo"—helps the information about the noun.

Sean es un estudiante bien educado. What is Sean like? "bien educado" —helps the adjective.

El médico vive en esta casa. El médico vive allí. What do we substitute in the second sentence? The place where the doctor lives (indicating with a gesture).

Example 4

Peter, mi amigo, viene de visita a mi casa. Trae una patineta especial. Con la patineta él puede correr, saltar y hacer muchas piruetas. Cuando él viene a mi casa nosotros nos divertimos. Me gusta mucho que Peter venga a mi casa.

Example of how this passage can be modified:

Peter, mi **mejor** amigo, viene **hoy** a mi casa. Trae una patineta **muy** especial. Con la patineta él puede correr **rápidamente**, saltar y hacer **muchas** piruetas. Cuando él viene a mi casa nosotros **siempre** nos divertimos. Me gusta **mucho** que Peter venga a mi casa.

Gender and number are another matter of great importance in the sentence. In this aspect Spanish bestows a feminine or masculine soul to things. Starting in fourth grade the correcting of these differences is very important, to raise the student's consciousness of them.

The examples given below help the students to have greater clarity. With drawings or real objects, we help the student to distinguish the gender and number of the noun in relation to and in agreement with the adjective and the article.

Example 5

La camisa—las camisas.

La camisa es blanca—las camisas son blancas.

El vestido—los vestidos.

El vestido es _____, los vestidos son _____ (the student adds the color.)

Then we ask why it is"azules" and not "azul." And they deduce the rule.

Then we can say: "The shirt is yellow," and the children have to translate into Spanish.

Then we go on to the plural.

They write these exercises in their notebooks. To complete the examples a volunteer writes the phrase or phrases on the board. The students correct, the teacher directs. You can also use short paragraphs from some familiar reading. The students then can create their own examples guided by the teacher.

On his exposition of the the relationship of person / noun / adjective / verb, Steiner expresses that grammar tells us that there are nouns. Nouns are names of objects, that in a certain way are self-contained in space. It is significant that we should find such objects in our lives. All things that can be expressed through nouns awaken our consciousness to our independence as human beings. On learning to name things with nouns we distinguish ourselves from the world around us. On calling an object "table" or "chair" we separate ourselves from the table and the chair; we are here, the table and the chair are there. It is totally different to describe things with adjectives. When we say: *the table is blue*, I am expressing something that unites me with the table. The characteristic that I perceive unites me with it. When I name something with a noun, I disassociate myself from it; when I describe it with an adjective, I become one with the object. Thus, the development of our consciousness takes place in our relationship with things when we address them. If I pronounce the verbal phrase, *the man writes,* not only do I unite myself with the being about whom I have referred the verb, I also do with him what he is doing in his physical body. I do what he does, my ego does what he does. When I enunciate a verb, my ego joins his ego, in what the physical body of the other person is doing. I unite my ego with the physical body of the other when I enunciate a verb. Our listening, especially with verbs, is always in reality a participation.

Fifth Grade

In fifth grade we continue with the work begun in fourth, and from this point on one can use a reader. Interweaving reading with activities and exercises, the student continues to be guided toward an understanding of grammar and the structure of the language.

1. The teacher can briefly introduce what the reading is about.
2. The class reads. We can begin with choral reading led by the teacher.
3. Recapitulation of the reading based on oral questions from the teacher. This is an opportunity to work on new vocabulary, writing it on the board and creating new sentences.

4. We read again emphasizing the pronunciation of the language to obtain better comprehension.

5. The reading can be done in pairs, or the teacher assigns paragraphs to different students. After all these exercises, the majority, if not all the students, understand the reading, and are familiar with the vocabulary and are ready to answer the questions in writing, thus reinforcing spelling. The questions can be copied on the board or photocopied on paper. The student will answer the questions in his notebook, then the teacher will formulate them again and the student will answer what he has written.

(Here the answers can be copied on the board or done orally.)

It is important to correct the written work of the student.

6. Re-telling: The students will tell about the reading in their own words, without the intervention of the teacher. The teacher can again extract the new vocabulary that the more advanced stu dents have brought to the re-telling, and review it.

7. a) A similar composition can be written with the help of every body. The teacher writes on the board as the student offers sent ences.

b) Students can work in pairs, telling the reading to each other or answering questions previously written.

8. The students should create their own story related to the reading, following it as a model. Then the teacher has to correct the student's story. It can be read or left as a written exercise.

By Means of Readings the Following Can Be Worked On:

1. The formation of sentences and the recognition of the elements that make up a sentence.

2. The grammar rules of each element of a sentence.

After studying this and bringing it to awareness, the student will carry out step number 8. It is advisable to focus gradually on each point, and apply it in oral and written exercises. In this way the student progressively internalizes and memorizes the rules.

Although all elements of sentence formation are worked on, in fifth grade the emphasis is on verbs.

1. The indicative mood of the present tense in its three conjugations (-ar, -er, -ir) of the regular verbs, their formation and usage.

2. The indicative mood of the present tense of the most common irregular verbs, in particular the differences between "ser" and "estar."

The presentation of the reflexive verbs in the present tense.

The best moment to work on reflexive verbs is during the review of daily routines. The teacher should prepare a reading or rhyme for presentation and then develop a series of oral and written exercises that will reinforce the learning.

Example 1

A las 7:00 de la mañana me despierto y me levanto.

A las 7:30 de la mañana me desayuno.

A las 8:00 de la mañana me voy a la escuela.

A las 12:30 del mediodía almuerzo.

A las 2:30 de la tarde salgo de la escuela.

A las 4:00 de la tarde preparo mi tarea.

A las 5:00 de la tarde practico mi violín.

A las 6:30 de la tarde ceno.

A las 9:00 de la noche me acuesto.

A las 10:00 de la noche viene el sueño.

This is repeated chorally, questions are asked, the new vocabulary is presented. Among all the students a similar rhyme with their real activities could be prepared. And then each one can prepare a personal routine. Afterwards it is divided into parts:

¿Qué hago cuando me levanto? voy al baño, me cepillo los dientes, me peino, me visto.

¿Qué hago en la escuela? Estudiar, aprender español, escribir, leer (Here the conjugations can be reviewed, "yo estudio, tú estudias . . . .")

¿Qué hago antes de dormir? me baño, me cambio, me cepillo los dientes . . .

By means of illustrations that reflect the different activities, the students learn the use of the vocabulary. Several games could also be played with these activities in order to expand toward the reflexives "se," "te," "nos."

Example 2: Mimicry

The student carries out an action and the teacher asks:

¿Qué hace él / ella?: él se peina.

Teacher: ¿Te peinas tú en la mañana?

Student: Sí / yo me peino en la mañana.

Teacher to the class: ¿Nos peinamos en la mañana?

Not only do we work on the reflexive forms but also with the conjugations in the present tense of other verbs, besides introducing the verb "hacer" subtly. With respect to the irregular verbs we can begin to work rhythmically.

Example 3: A Rhyme

Yo tengo, tú quieres, él dice, ella va, nosotros podemos, ellos dan, ellas saben,

tener, querer, decir, ser y estar
poder, dar, saber, ir y hacer
son acciones que me pueden ayudar
para hablar, para comunicar
muchas cosas que quiero expresar.
A ver, compañeros, repitamos sin parar:
Yo tengo, tú tienes . . .

Here several conjugations are repeated; one can begin with three. Short legends, descriptions of some activity done at the school or by the students, are very good tools for working on this theme. If we intersperse the study of the different cultural aspects of the Spanish-speaking world with the study of the language, we create a good balance in the teaching of Spanish. The practical use of a language is one of the reasons for teaching it, but it is not the total focus in Waldorf schools.

Imaginary Trips to the Spanish-speaking World

Example of an activity to relate cultural and historical aspects to language use.

A. General Objectives of the Activity

1. To show the student the different Spanish-speaking countries of the world.
2. To show the student that even though these countries share a com mon language, each one has its own identity and cultural charac teristics.
3. To sow a seed of interest in this beautiful Spanish-speaking world.
4. To open a door to future lessons in the upper grades, relating the Spanish-speaking world to the development of civilizations and of humanity.
5. To work in an entertaining and stimulating way in the learning areas of vocabulary enrichment, oral comprehension and expres sion, re-telling and reading, expression in writing, phonetics, and grammar.
6. To stimulate the development of appreciation for the arts, the folk lore, and cultures of the Spanish-speaking world.

B. Introduction for the Activity
1. The Spanish-speaking countries are presented and divided into three regions:

Europe: Spain
The Caribbean: Puerto Rico, Dominican Republic, Cuba
Latin America
México
Central America: Guatemala, El Salvador,
Honduras, Nicaragua, Costa Rica, Panamá.
South America: Venezuela, Colombia, Ecuador,
Perú, Chile, Bolivia, Paraguay, Uruguay, Argentina.

2. Presenting the geography of the Spanish-speaking world
Draw on the board the map of Latin America, the Caribbean, and Spain. If drawing this is not feasible, use a printed map. The student draws the map in her notebook. Name and locate on the map the Spanish-speaking countries. Name, locate by region, and color.

3. Have a short chat about different Spanish-speaking countries that the students may have visited. Encourage the students to ex press themselves in Spanish. In fifth grade they study botany, and in this block, the different zones of the globe are covered. One could begin the imaginary journeys visiting one of the geographic zones studied in class, for example: the Caribbean, or tropical zone. In each country visited, its geography, chief ag ricultural products, and flora and fauna are mentioned in a simple way and related to the activity that is being carried out.

C. Examples of countries to visit with the fifth grade and topics to cover:
The Caribbean:
Puerto Rico: Taíno culture. Legends: *Cómo nació el mar*, by Lulú De Lacre; *Atariba y Niguayona*, by Rohmer.
-Tropical forest — *El Yunque*
-African influence —*Carnaval de Vejigantes*
-Music: *La bamba*, African influence; *La danza*, Spanish influence; *La Plena* and *las Parrandas Navideñas*, Puerto Rican idiosyncracies.
Dominican Republic: agricultural products: coffee, cacao,tobacco
Music: the Dominican merengue
Cuba: agricultural product: tobacco and sugar.
Music: the guaracha

2. México
Since California shares a border with Mexico, a country to which it once belonged during a historical period, and

since the influence of Mexico is still strong in that state (as well as in others), it is of fundamental interest to study this neighboring country. Some topics to be studied are: emigration, agriculture, and celebrations such as "Cinco de mayo" and "Día de los Muertos." A good reading is the Aztec legend *Cómo vinimos al quinto mundo* by Rohmer and Achondo. There are also Mayan legends in *El rey colibrí* by Argentina Palacios and selections of the *Popol Vuh.*

South America
Perú: The origins of the Inca Empire should be briefly presented with the reading of the legends *Manco Cápac* and *La vara de oro* by Lulú De Lacré .

D. Creation of different situations and trips
In each country that we travel to, the student encounters different situations that she should resolve, such as:
-asking for tourist information and directions,
-crossing borders, showing the passport, and explaining the reason for the trip,
-taking different means of transportation, buying tickets,
-changing money from one's country to the national currency of the country being visited,
-looking for lodging,
-going to a restaurant and ordering food.

Below is a sample lesson:

IMAGINARY TRIP TO PUERTO RICO (everything is presented in Spanish).
Lesson 1. Trip by boat to Puerto Rico and visit to the Tibes Ceremonial Park, Taíno culture.
Materials: prepare the room beforehand with permission of the main lesson teacher. Place on a table artifacts representative of taína culture, such as "ditas," a stone with petroglyph, maracas, pictures, a carved "coquí" toad, a musical recording with sounds of the forest and the song of the coquí. Also a map of the world, and areas that need to be readied, except the desks and chairs, which are put in their places during the activity.
Upon the teacher's entrance, the students stand up.
Teacher: -¡Buenas tardes, quinto grado!
Students: -¡Buenas tardes, Señora Enid!

Teacher and students: recitation of the poem "Frente al mar."

Teacher and students: Song "Al tambor de la alegría"

Teacher: -Hoy viajaremos desde Newport Beach a Ponce en Puerto Rico, e iremos en barco. (Shows a small ship) Favor de colocar sus sillas mirando hacia la pared a su derecha (the teacher takes her seat and does what she is saying) — Siéntense cómodos, por favor.

The teacher goes to the map of the world, placed in the direction toward which they placed the chairs. She points out the route: Saldremos en breves momentos hacia Puerto Rico, navegaremos por el Océ ano Pacífico hasta llegar a Panamá, cruzaremos el Canal de Panamá, pasando el Mar Caribe, navegando cerca de las Islas de Jamaica, Haití, República Dominicana, hasta llegar a Puerto Rico (Ten minutes have passed up to this point).

Por favor, ahora deben comprar sus boletos para el viaje, en silencio pasar hacia la caseta donde venden los boletos, luego, favor de abordar el barco. (While this is being explained with pertinent gestures, the teacher sits in the chair of a student, gets up, and walks toward the desk where a sign reads: VENTA DE BOLETOS, and says out loud):

-Un boleto para Puerto Rico, por favor (indicates that the class should repeat, takes a ticket, and says):

-Gracias (she returns to the chair, sits down, and asks): -¿Listos?

They reply: -Listos.

(One of them goes to sell the tickets; if there are students who speak Spanish well, they can be asked to help out)

-Pueden comenzar a comprar sus boletos, favor de hacer fila de uno en uno.

Dialogue at the ticket window:

Teacher: -¡Buenas tardes! ¿En qué puedo servirlo?

Student: -Un boleto a Puerto Rico, por favor.

Teacher (handing over the ticket) -¡Que tenga buen viaje!

Student: -Gracias.

(This takes about five minutes).

(When they have all bought their tickets, one of them goes to the map again and says):

-Bienvenidos todos a bordo.

Teacher: ¿Adónde vamos?

Student: Vamos a Puerto Rico.

Teacher: ¿En qué vamos? (showing the boat)

Student: Vamos en barco.

Teacher: ¿Por dónde navegaremos?

Student: Navegaremos por el Océano Pacífico.

Teacher: Cuando lleguemos a Panamá, ¿qué canal cruzaremos?

Student: Cruzaremos el canal de Panamá.

Teacher: Al cruzar el canal de Panamá, ¿llegaremos a qué mar?

Student: Llegaremos al Mar Caribe.

Teacher: ¿Pasando cerca de las Islas?

Student: Jamaica, Haití, República Dominicana.

Teacher: ¿Llegando a?

Student: Puerto Rico.

Teacher: Bienvenidos a Puerto Rico, hemos llegado a Ponce (showing on the map). Puerto Rico es una isla tropical en el Caribe. Su idioma oficial es el español. Los primeros habitantes de Puerto Rico fueron los indígenas Taínos. Estos indios trabajaban la piedra pulida, los grabados en piedra y prendas en caracoles.Utilizaban la higuera para hacer ditas e instrumentos musicales como las maracas y el güiro, lo hacían con un calabazo alargado, creando su raspe de madera. (show artifacts and pictures representative of what is being said). (Up to this point about 20-25 minutes have passed).

—Hoy iremos a visitar el Centro Ceremonial Indígenas Tibes. Tenemos que prepararnos para la jornada. (Take out a small backpack and from it a bottle of water, a handkerchief, a map, a flashlight. While doing this, signal to the class to sit down and pretend to prepare their own backpacks. On finishing this, put on the backpack and ask) —¿Listos?

—Ahora con cuidado, montémonos en las canoas (accompanied by gestures). Rememos a un mismo compás todos por el río que nos llevará hasta el Tibes. (Play short instrumental music that has the sound of the "coquí", the sound of the river bed, and that of the birds of Puerto Rico. The class could begin to try to reproduce these sounds.)

—Hemos llegado al Tibes, debemos abrirnos pasos, coloca tu silla sobre la mesa y empujemos las mesas hasta el final del salón (accompany with gestures). (30 minutes have now passed).

—Síganme de uno en uno (walk around the room forming a circle in the middle, and have them sit down on the floor; when they are seated, the teacher goes to the magic place, puts on a cloak and picks up the maracas.

—Soy el Gran Cacique Agüeybaná, bienvenidos al Tibes, sitio sagrado de los indígenas Taínos, y quiero contarles una historia. (Briefly tell the legend of *Cómo nació el mar,* and at the end have the class stand up).

—Ahora deseo que me acompañen en esta pequeña danza al dios del mar. (Play instrumental music and carry out physical movements to the rhythm of the music; the students imitate). Gracias por su visita al Tibes, vayan todos en paz. (35-40 minutes have passed).

Indicate that the activity will continue in the next class. Tell them to go silently to their tables and put them in their places, thus ending the day's lesson. They arrange the tables and chairs, of course, talking and making some noise; when they are more or less ready, ring a little bell to signal for quiet, and begin the closing verse:

—Gracias a la vida, por haberme dado tanto, me ha dado el arte de aprender, el cual estoy usando, y aprendo español, para poder comunicarme, con el mundo hispano, en su hermoso lenguaje.

Specific objectives for lessons 1 and 2
1, The student will answer questions such as:
    a. ¿Es Puerto Rico una isla tropical?
      ¿Dónde está Puerto Rico?
      ¿Qué idioma hablan en Puerto Rico?
      ¿Cómo se llamaban los indígenas de Puerto Rico?

    b. and questions related to:
    —the route taken to get to Puerto Rico, naming the ocean, sea, canal, and a minimum of three countries of the five mentioned.

2. The student will have the opportunity to see and know about some objects representative of the Taíno Indians, such as ditas, maracas, stones with petroglyph, and in addition, will have the opportunity to listen to the sound of the "coquí," an animal that is found only in Puerto Rico, and to see an image of the little animal, carved in stone.

3. The student will experience a simple situation of how to ask for a ticket and will use courtesy phrases.

4. The student will listen to the legend *Cómo nació el mar* and will answer questions related to it, creating the chronological order of the legend, and reaffirming or clarifying the oral comprehension of it.

5. The student will work on oral comprehension of the language, united with gestures and the imaginary experience, which include the sounds of the river, the "coquí" and the birds in the woods, and dancing the dance of the god of the sea, all of which will enable him to express orally and narrate his imaginary trip in simple terms. The student will execute commands in Spanish, which are given during the activity, such as: "toma tu silla y colócala mirando a la pared que está a tu derecha."

6. The student will copy in his Spanish notebook a summary of the activity carried out, making a drawing that represents the activity in general, the part that he enjoyed the most, or a representation of what he learned about the legend that was heard and discussed.

Lesson 2: An Imaginary Trip to Puerto Rico
    Teacher:—¡Buenos días, quinto grado!

Students:–¡Buenos días, Señor / Señora . . .!
All together: Poem "Frente al mar" and song "Al tambor de la alegría."

1. A talk about the activity in general is begun. The teacher directs the talk with questions such as those given in the example below, and prepares a summary on the board.

Example:

Teacher: ¿Quién puede comenzar a contar el viaje imaginario que comenzamos en la clase anterior? ¿adónde viajamos?, ¿es Puerto Rico una isla tropical?, ¿dónde está Puerto Rico?, ¿qué idioma hablan en Puerto Rico?, ¿en qué viajamos a Puerto Rico?, ¿qué ruta tomamos para llegar de California a Puerto Rico?, Cuando llegamos a Puerto Rico, ¿con qué preparamos una mochila?, ¿en qué navegamos por el río?, ¿qué escuchaste durante el viaje en canoa?, ¿qué pasó al llegar al Parque Ceremonial Indígena Tibes?, ¿de qué trata la leyenda Cómo nació el mar?, ¿quié n es Yayá?, ¿quié n es Yayael?, en qué se convierten los huesos de Yayael?, ¿qué pasa luego?, ¿cómo nació el mar según la leyenda?, después de escuchar la leyenda, ¿qué hicimos?

2. A short summary of the answers to these questions on activity #1 is written on the board.

Example:

"Viajamos a Puerto Rico, una isla tropical en el Caribe. Viajamos en barco, por el Océano Pacífico, hasta Panamá. Cruzamos el Canal de Panamá, llegando al Mar Caribe. Pasamos cerca de las islas de Jamaica, Cuba, Haití, República Domincana, llegando a Puerto Rico. Luego, preparamos nuestras mochilas con agua, un mapa, una linterna de mano, y viajamos en canoa por el río hacia el Tibes, escuchando la melodía del coquí y los pájaros en el bosque. Al llegar al Parque Indígena, sitio sagrado de los taínos, el cacique no narra la leyenda Cómo nació el mar, y al final bailamos una danza en honor al dios del mar." (deliberately use verbs without subject pronouns, a point that will be taken up later).

The students copy the summary in their notebooks, and as homework, they make one or several drawings representing the activity in general, the part they most enjoyed, or the representation of what they got from the legend.

End the class by indicating that we will continue our trip to Puerto Rico, reading about Niguayona, a Taíno boy. In the reading the methods previously explained are followed. After the reading comes the re-telling, the different areas of grammatical focus, the application of them, and above all, talk, talk, talk with the students. In the next class it is important to ask for the folders or notebooks to correct their work.

In this fashion the language in its totality, together with the culture of the countries visited, are worked on. The student tells his experience using the present tense, even though it is a past experience. This material can be used to review grammatical aspects such as agreement of the article, noun, and adjective in gender and number; the structure of the sentence, the position of the adjective in Spanish, and the conjugation of regular and irregular verbs in the present.

Sixth Grade

At this age the feeling forces, which have been gradually cultivated through the will in previous years, are going to begin penetrating the thinking of the student. It is of great importance to have appropriate enriching material that will nurture and help the student in his growth as an individual. It is essential to have continuity in the learning of grammar, reviewing and expanding previous knowledge, and introducing new elements. One must keep in mind that grammar can be presented in a real context applicable to the student's surroundings. This is why one can work better if the student can get a picture of what is being presented. In this way his soul is freed and will grow in the future. In sixth grade we study the language using as a basis short stories, re-telling, readings and interpretations, and having the students express orally and in writing their personal impressions toward the material. It is advisable to avoid translations, although the students can use a dictionary to look up key words. In this grade we study Spain and the way in which it expanded toward America. Using the reading material, recapitulation, and discussion, oral and written exercises, and the writing of brief compositions, the class can acquire new vocabulary and continue with the study and analysis of grammar. Dialogues and conversations arising from the reading materials acquire greater importance from now on.

Steiner recommends that the teacher speak about everything connected with the customs and conditions of the people who speak the foreign language.

These topics will stimulate the use of the language as a means of communication, while at the same time the students are applying the knowledge they have already acquired. After the reading , using the method presented for the previous grades, the teacher can create a situation related to it.

Example 1 : Create a situation where the student has to work with descriptions and personal information.

1. The situation is created.
2. The student should work out a minimum of eight questions for interacting with a classmate.
3. Each student copies or writes his questions in the notebook.
4. Pairs or groups are chosen for working together, the questions are gone over, and the answers obtained are copied down.
5. The information obtained is reported.
6. Corrections are carried out with the general participation of the class.

Conjugations of regular verbs in the present tense must be absolutely clear to all students, even the new ones. Also the conjugations in present tense of the irregular verbs: **ir, ser, estar, tener, decir, querer, hacer, y poder.** To this end the teacher should create oral and written exercises using work sheets that help the student in this process.

Some examples of activities for this goal:

Example 2: Irregular Verbs "ir," "tener," "querer."

We are going on a short trip. For the trip we can only take one object or thing, and we can only do one action. Choose where you are going, what you are taking, and what action you want to do, as well as: where the other passengers are going, what they are taking, and what they want to do on the trip.

Países	Objetos o cosas	Acciones
Puerto Rico	un pantalón	bailar
España	una camiseta	cantar
Cuba	unos zapatos	comer
México	unas sandalias	vivir
Costa Rica	unas gafas	jugar
Perú	un sombrero	escribir
Colombia	un libro	hablar
Venezuela	un lápiz	pensar
Argentina	un papel	gozar
El Salvador	una flauta	estudiar
Chile	una guitarra	dibujar
Paraguay	un violín	caminar
Uruguay	un cello	correr
República Dominicana	un mapa	escuchar
Guatemala	una flor	tocar
Honduras	un teléfono	imaginar

Ecuador	una radio	comprar
Bolivia	un reloj	beber
Nicaragua	un refresco	admirar

Yo voy a _____, tengo _____ y quiero_____

Tú vas a _____, tienes _____ y quieres_____

Èl va a _____, tiene _____ y quiere_____

Ella va a_____, tiene_____ y quiere_____

Nosotros vamos a_____,tenemos_____ y queremos _____

Nosotras vamos a_____,tenemos_____ y queremos _____

Ellos van a _____,tienen_____ y quieren _____

Explanation and Application of this Exercise:

1. The teacher prepares three groups of cards: the countries, the objects, and the actions.

2. She writes on the blackboard:

Yo voy a_____, tengo _____ y quiero_____.

3. She distributes a card from each group to each student.
4. The student has to fill in the blank spaces based on the cards.
5. Each student reads aloud what he has filled out.
6. In case of an error, the same student who read has to correct himself; if he doesn't succeed, another can help him.
7. The cards include the personal pronouns **yo, tú, él, ella, nosotros, nosotras, ellos,** and **ellas.**

Example 3: Exercise Based on Reading and Questions. The Verb QUERER.

¡Cuántas cosas queremos nosotros!

Hay un grupo de amigos que está hablando de todas las cosas que quieren. —En el futuro yo quiero ser veterinaria dice Natalia. Juanita dice que ella quiere vivir en el campo y tener una granja con muchos animales. José Antonio quiere viajar. Por todo el mundo. Islabel quiere escribir cuentos para niños. Gabriel y Margarita quieren ser músicos, y Josefina quiere ser maestra. —Y tú, ¿qué quieres ser? —le pregunta Natalia a Miguel. —Yo quiero soñar, comer y bailar responde. Todos nosotros reímos.

1. ¿Qué quiere Natalia?
2. ¿Qué quieren Gabriel y Margarita?
3. ¿Qué quiere José Antonio?
4. ¿Qué quiere Isabel y Josefina?

5. ¿Qué quiere Miguel?
6. ¿Qué quieres tú?

Example 4: Exercise with the Verbs PODER, DECIR, AND SABER:

Yo puedo _____, yo digo_____, yo sé _____.

Tú puedes _____, tú dices_____, tú sabes_____.

Èl puede_____, él dice_____, él sabe_____.

Ella puede_____, ella dice_____, ella sabe_____.

Nosotros podemos_____, decimos_____, sabemos_____.

Nosotras podemos_____, decimos_____, sabemos_____.

Ellos pueden _____, dicen_____, saben_____.

Ellas pueden_____, dicen_____, saben_____.

hablar	hola	hablar español
cantar	adiós	contar historias
bailar	hasta luego	lavar la ropa
comer	buenos días	cocinar arroz
vivir	buenas tardes	hacer ejercicios
escribir	buenas noches	llamar por teléfono
leer	¿cómo estás?	pedir permiso
pensar	¿qué tal?	geografía
gozar	con permiso	patinar sobre hielo
viajar	lo siento	montar a caballo
estudiar	muchas gracias	limpiar el cuarto
escuchar	listos	sembrar árboles
correr	de nada	pedir disculpas

This exercise is also good for pointing out the use of two verbs in a row, where the first is conjugated and the second is not, staying in the infinitive.

Although the students are familiar with possessive adjectives, in sixth grade they gain a greater clarity in the use of them. Here too, after oral practice, written work sheets can be used, prepared by the teacher based on the oral work; or one can use exercise booklets.

It is important for the student to recognize and practice the demonstrative adjectives and their uses. An example:

1. Take several concrete objects from the class, such as pencils, books, chalk, etc.
2. Place them at three different distances in relation to the students.
3. Group them together or separately for presenting the singular and the plural.

The teacher points to and expresses an object orally in its three distances: "este lápiz, ese lápiz, aquel lápiz."

The students repeat. The objects are grouped together to present the plural and one could use "la libreta," for presenting the feminine gender. After the presentation, other examples are carried out, in which the student will determine which demonstrative to use. As a final point, the uses can be deduced. Example:

—este / esta / esto — to refer to something that is near the speaker.

—ese / esa / eso — to refer to something a little farther.

—aquel / aquella / aquello—for what is much farther away.

During the lesson the teacher should try to intersperse peculiarities of expression, the richness of proverbs, and idiomatic phrases,from different places from fifth grade on. Examples:

> "No cruces el río antes de llegar a él."
> "Cada loco con su tema."
> "El que está libre de culpa que tire la primera piedra."
> "Oh, oh pero bueno" (Dominican Repulic)
> "Óyeme chico" (Cuba)
> "Qué chévere" (Puerto Rico)
> "Pero che" (Argentina)

There is a tremendous number of expressions, and students love to be able to use them and repeat them.

In sixth grade we can establish a system for looking up words in the dictionary. Example: after a reading, a list of key words is made up (no more than 10). The student has to look up their meaning for homework and construct simple sentences using them.The next day they are presented in class, and if a word has several meanings, we point out which is the most appropriate for what one wants to communicate.

Sixth grade is the continuation and integration of everything learned in previous years. It is a conscious review of the language. The foundations should stay firm to progress further in the acquisition and practical use of the language. The student should handle a knowledge of the following grammatical elements (and their application in conversation):

- The formation and use of regular verbs in the present tense

- The present of irregular verbs: **tener, ser, estar, ir, dar, ver, querer, salir, venir, decir, jugar.**

- The use of reflexive verbs

- The agreement of gender and number between article, noun, and adjective
- The use of possessive and demonstrative adjectives
- Idiomatic expressions with "hacer" and weather; "tener" and "tener que"

Seventh Grade

Obviously the challenge in the upper grades is to keep the language alive. For this purpose situations can be created where the students can carry on conversations between themselves and with the teacher. Debates, dialogues, and conversations should reflect the content of what we want to teach, facilitating the forming of conclusions. For this reason reading is highly advisable, to create dialogues, debates, and conversations. "In seventh and eighth grades one should put emphasis on reading and on observing the nature of the language through the study of sentences. The students should encounter typical aspects of the life and activities of the people whose language they are learning. Printed material should be the basis for practice, and through narration they should practice expressing themselves in the foreign language." (***Curriculum for Waldorf Schools,*** Stockmeyer).

Information to be presented on the pre-Columbian cultures and on present-day life should be short and simple. These topics can also be used for the study of grammar (verb tenses) and of the sentence. In seventh grade verb conjugations in the present tense are reviewed, and the simple past, the imperfect, and if possible the future, are introduced.

For the review of verbs in the present tense, it is possible to create a chat on personal likes, what they expect from the Spanish class, the introduction of new students, and other opportune topics. One could present a funny reading like *El precio de la fama* in which a South American boa snake pays the price of being famous with indigestion. The reading prepares the way for going on and working on the simple past and the imperfect of regular and irregular verbs.

When presenting a reading like this, the teacher needs to prepare her students. The reading should be presented in a simple, oral form. If appropriate, bring pictures or illustrations with details that you wish to emphasize, just a few imaginative ones, enough to create interest so the activity can be carried out. Then go on to the reading, the recapitulation, and the presentation of the new vocabulary. When the student understands the reading, the grammatical aspects can be worked on.

Examples for Teaching the Simple Past Tense:
1. Take from the reading several sentences have regular verbs, and write them on the board,
2. Point to and underline the verbs,
3. Take the first verb,
4. Begin the analysis using as a basis questions like:
   What does the action indicate?
   What is the infinitive?
   Conjugate the verb in the present indicative tense.
   Change the action to the present in the sentence.
   Point out who is doing the action and replace the person with the pronoun.
   Write the verb with its subject pronoun, in the infinitive.
   Point out and write the rest of the conjugation of the verb using the other pronouns.
   Make up questions where the student answers using the verb correctly.
5. Take another example and repeat the previous steps.
6. Classify the verbs according to their infinitive ending.
7. Write all their forms in the simple past.
8. Encourage the students to extract the rule for its formation and copy it in their notebooks.

For practice, the students should give examples, write, and tell about some past experience. They can also work in pairs, changing a paragraph written in the present to the past tense. Narration activities should be worked on throughout the year. In teaching the past tense of verbs, some teachers also present the imperfect. You should choose the alternative that feels most comfortable to you.

Below we present an example for working on both forms together. As an introduction a little story can be created to explain the use of the past in a pleasant way: with actions in the past you can find two paths to follow. One where you carry out an action and when you tell it, it was completed, it's final. And on the other path, even though you tell a story that happened in the past, it indicates that perhaps you repeated it, perhaps not; who knows?

Example:
1. Action that was completed, it is final:
   "El sábado yo **estuve** en un restaurante cerca de la playa. **Miré** el mar y **pensé** : ¡qué hermoso! **Comí** pescado y **bebí** limonada. ¡Qué tarde agradable **pasé** ! Cuando **regresé** a mi casa **escribí** todo lo que **pasó** ese día."

2. Habitual action:

"Todos los sábados yo estaba en un restaurante cerca de la playa. **Miraba** el mar y **pensaba**: ¡Qué hermoso! **Comía** pescado y **bebía** limonada. ¡Qué tardes agradables **pasaba**! Cuando **regresaba** a mi casa **escribía** todo lo que **pasaba** esos días."

How do we form these actions?

1. We take the actions of the regular verbs in their infinitive form:
   Mirar, pensar, comer, beber, pasar, escribir
2. We take an example of each conjugation –ar, -er, -ir
   -ar: mirar   -er: comer   -ir: escribir
3. Conjugate the examples in the present tense (mirar, comer, escribir)
4. Give examples in both past tenses:
   Yo miré , miraba   yo comí, comía   yo escribí, escribía
5. The verbs with their complete conjugations in the past are written on the board:

> yo miré , miraba
> tú miraste, mirabas
> él miró, miraba
> nosotras miramos, mirábamos
> ellos miraron, miraban
>
> yo comí, comía
> tú comiste, comías
> él comió, comía
> nosotros comimos, comíamos
> ellas comieron, comían
>
> yo escribí, escribía
> tú escribiste, escribías
> él escribió, escribía
> nosotros escribimos, escribíamos
> ellos escribieron, escribían

6. Extract the rules for forming these tenses and copy them in note books.

7. Other examples are given to guide the student toward noticing the differences between the two past tenses:

"Siempre **cantaba** en la mañana, pero el lunes **canté** todo el día."

"Generalmente Juan **llegaba** temprano, pero el martes **llegó** tarde."

By using examples as a basis, the student should deduce that the simple past (pretente) expresses a specific time when an action happens (ayer . . . , el lunes . . .) and the imperfect is used to indicate past actions that are habitual and not enclosed in a specific time (siempre . . . , generalmente . . . todos los días, . . . , mientras . . . .).

The students will carry out examples using both forms.

Later they can be asked to tell or write about a past experience using either of the forms or combinations of them.

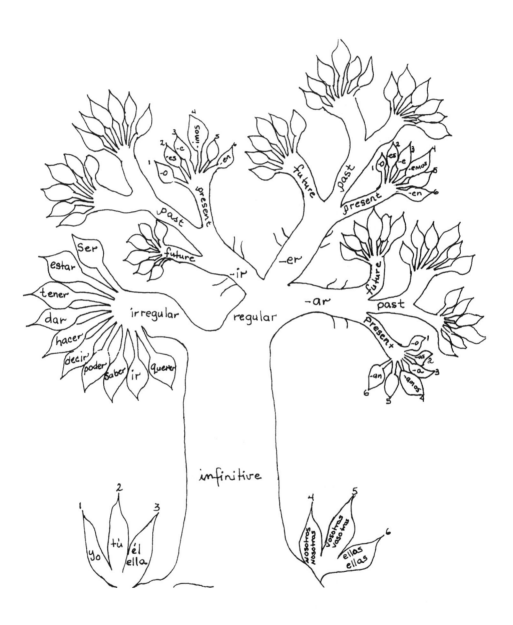

In order to present the irregular verbs after choral recitation of the ones to be learned, we can use another reading selection, either created by the teacher or an existing one. When presenting an already existing text, we need to keep in mind its complexity: it is important to study it and be discerning so as to present it as clearly as possible.

Other grammatical elements to be worked on are the direct object pronouns: lo, los, la, las. Once again we can present them with real examples. Without further explanation the students will have to listen attentively to be able to establish the rule.

Tengo un libro. Yo lo tengo.
Miro a Lauren. Yo la miro.
Compro dos faldas. Yo las compro.
Compra unos zapatos. Alex los compra.
Mi madre mira una película. Mi madre la mira.
Mi padre escribe un reporte. Mi padre lo escribe.
Mis abuelos compran una casa. Mis abuelos la compran.
Yo compro unos pantalones y una falda. Yo los compro.

After giving these examples, the class has to extract the rule. In this case it is easy for most of them. Having established these pronouns, we go on to teach more direct object pronouns.

Rule: A direct object pronoun receives the action directly. (I have it). It comes before the verb in Spanish.

The next class day during the re-telling phase, we go through a recapitulation with some examples, and afterwards we repeat the rule.

The focus during the seventh grade is enabling the student, after several years of instruction, to understand and to express himself in practical situations. On the basis of readings and examples drawn from them, and real situations created in the class, the teacher, during the lesson, should:

1, Carry out a good review of the regular verbs in the present tense.
2, Present and review the past tenses of regular verbs.
3. Review the uses of "ser" and "estar."
4. Present and review the past tenses of irregular verbs:
    a. preferir, empezar, querer (e, ie)
    b. poder, dormir, volver (o, ue)
    c. hacer, traer, venir, salir, poner
    d. saber, conocer
5. Work on the simple past of the basic irregular verbs:
    Ser, estar, tener, ir . . .
6. Review the reflexive verbs.
7. Review possessive and demonstrative adjectives.
8. Present the direct object pronouns.

We need to be aware that in the upper grades, and particularly in the seventh, different levels of comprehension and use of the language are going to modify the class dynamics. The language teacher may often find himself with a considerable number of new students whose experiences with the language have been uneven. To this we must add the impact on a caused by a change of faculty. These conditions compromise the development and learning of the language. The teaching staff should search for solutions and support within the institutional framework, to create practical approaches and vehicles of communication among colleagues and with the parents of the students. Some solutions that have been put into practice are:

Divide into groups by ability in the seventh and eighth grades.

Private tutoring as a requirement for admission to the school in sixth, seventh, and eighth grades.

Separate lessons for students with difficulties, so that they may reach a basic level.

If he succeeds in putting into practice any of these solutions, the teacher will be able to work in better conditions, helping the student to achieve a certain mastery of the language. Otherwise, the teacher will have to prepare and design a course that covers the basic needs of each level.

Eighth Grade
Introduction

At this age children wish to experience and come to grips with the material by themselves. They try to penetrate into the why and the how of the language. The apprenticeship that they have been acquiring in previous years and the reasons behind the grammatical forms will appear as pieces in a puzzle being put together with logic, while the teacher creates situations and practical lessons that clarify concepts and rules. When the teacher unites examples and grammatical explanations with personal situations of the students, the language gains another meaning. Precisely for these reasons, the teacher design lessons so that the student will take an active part.

Ideally the instructor will begin with a reading or recitation of a poem, the recapitulation of the previous lesson, clarification or presentation of new examples in case of doubts, and then new material. Below are some examples of grammatical topics to be covered.

A. Indirect object pronouns

This presentation usually takes several days. As a first step the students receive practical oral examples. The objective is to establish the use of the pronouns "me," "te," "le." The students have to know and use with fluency the conjugation of basic regular and iregular verbs in the simple past, as well as the vocabulary used in the examples.

First step

    1. Orally and in Spanish the teacher takes a book and says:

        "Yo doy el libro a Cara. Le doy el libro."

        "Cara le da el libro a Dylan, y Dylan me da el libro a mí ."

        ¿Qué pasa en estos ejemplos? Escuchen otra vez. (I again repeat the above but changing to a hat in my hand. The students translate into English and answer me). "to her, to him, to me." Then I write the example on the board. I again ask: Who receives the action? They answer: "ella, Cara." And in the second case? They answer: "él, Dylan."

    Then I write the second example: Cara le da el libro a Dylan. "To me, to him, to her."

The students then extract the rule by saying: When it refers to her or to him, we use "le" and to me, "me." The word "to" or "for" may be expressed or implied in English. Because they tell "to whom" or "for whom" something is done, we call them indirect object pronouns.

They will then write the rule in their notebooks. Let's look at some more examples.

Second Step

In the next step the teacher will give the students examples in English. They have to translate:

Yesterday, I gave my homework to my teacher. He told me that it was not that good. I looked at him sadly, and I sat down. My friend Mara gave me her book. His book was perfect and it made me feel happy. When I finished it, I gave it back to Mara, but she forgot and then she exclaimed: "Cara, give me my book." Quickly I answered: "But I just gave it to you, don't you remember? Then, I went to my teacher's desk, and I talked to him about some corrections in my book.

After finishing the translation, we correct the paragraph, focusing on the direct and indirect object pronouns.

In the following class, we go over what we learned. The last example can also serve as a review of the ones we did the previous day. The class translates and again establishes the rule.

The next step is teaching "te," "nos," and "les."

Let's look at the following example:

El maestro nos dio la tarea de Cara como ejemplo. Nos pareció una tarea muy buena y aplaudimos. Cara empezó a toser de nervios y le dimos un vaso de agua. Ella bebió y me dio el vaso vacío. "Cara, ¿ te damos otro vaso lleno de agua?" le preguntamos. "No, gracias", respondió Cara, "les estoy agradecida. Ahora les explicaré cómo hice la tarea." A todos nos pareció perfecto. Al final el professor dijo: "Cara, te daré una nota excelente por tu contribución."

After the students have translated these examples into English, they deduce the rule. "To me," "to her," "to him," "to you," "to us," "to them." And they copy the following:

The direct object pronoun receives the action directly and comes before the verb. The indirect object pronoun tells for whom or to whom something is done.

In the following lesson we recapitulate with specific examples that will be translated from English into Spanish:

> I gave them the book.
> My mother gave me a message.
> I told you about my friend.
> She gave us a sweater, etc.

After presenting the vocabulary related to a visit to a doctor, this can be a good example for practicing direct and indirect object pronouns: "me," "te,", "nos," "le," "les." Let us look at the following example:

Tengo gripe. Ayer fui al médico y me recetó unos antibióticos. Yo le dije que me dolía la garganta y la cabeza también. El médico me dio la receta y mi madre le preguntó que cuántas pastillas tenía que tomar. Nos dijo que dos pastillas al día. Nos dio la receta y después me preguntó por mi hermano menor. Yo le dije que él estaba en la escuela. Mi madre le respondió que estaba bien. El mé dico me dio los buenos días y nosotros le dimos las gracias por la consulta.

A. Irregular verbs in the simple past
Exercise that integrates material previously studied.

María camina al restaurante. Ella llega y ordena algo para comer y beber. Ella espera a una amiga por 15 minutos. Su amiga llega y saluda. María y Juana hablan un rato. Juana le pregunta a María por su familia. María le responde que están muy bien. Luego ellas van a la tienda. María compra una camisa para Juana.

María regresa a su casa en autobús. Ella para primero en un mercado, compra comida para preparar la cena. Una vez en casa, mientras su hija toca la guitarra y escucha música, María cocina y limpia la casa.

El tío Pepe llega de sorpresa. Èl es profesor en la universidad. Pepe escribe una bonita poesía para su sobrina Ana.

Cuando llega su marido todos comen la cena. Todos exclaman ¡Qué delicia! cuando ven el pastel sobre la mesa.

This is a simple story that will be augmented with the vocabulary already known by the student. The idea is to add to this story everything previously learned. This reading can be used in several classes to take advantage of it to the fullest extent. It is better to do it first orally, at least the first paragraph; then the teacher should write on the board as the students continue adding to it. This helps the student understand the assignment. Here are some examples that can be added to the story.

1. Date, season, weather and time.
2. Describe María and Juana physically. Their age, profession, nationality, what they like to do or not like.
3. What María is eating and drinking in the restaurant.
4. Write a dialogue between María and the waiter.
5. Describe María's family, and add grandparents, aunts and uncles, and cousins.
6. Describe the shops where Mar'a makes purchases, and the products she buys.
7. Write dialogues between them and the sellers.
8. Describe Uncle Pepe and what he does.
9. Describe María's husband.

Example with modifications:

"Es lunes 3 de enero. Hace frío y hay mucho viento. Son las 12:00 del mediodía y es la hora del almuerzo. María tiene hambre y camina al restaurante italiano. Ella es una muchacha alta y bonita. Tiene el pelo castaño y los ojos verdes. Ella es española pero vive en California. Tiene 20 años y trabaja en una oficina. A María le gusta comer y cocinar, pero no le gusta mucho practicar deportes."

Grammar activities to be carried out with the original story:

1. Underline the verbs and write the infinitives.
2. Put the story in the simple past.
3. Use a different subject for the story.
4. Change the definite articles to indefinite articles.
5. Add an adjective to each noun.
6. Add adverbs.
7. Use direct object pronouns.

Steiner observed that one should put the greatest emphasis on reading, observing the character of the language through the study of sentences. Moreover, the children should encounter the typical elements in the life and activities of the people whose language they are studying. Written material should be the basis for practice, and through re-telling, the students should express themselves in the foreign language. Furthermore, he added that it is necessary to stress the character of the language by analyzing sentences, without forgetting the importance of getting into the spirit of history.

The teacher should pace the activities according to the needs of the class. The method should be clear and precise, though flexible to accommodate the different student levels. Not-with-standing the existence of a program and plan of study, one should not rush the class if the students are not able to keep up with it. It is better to cover less ground, making sure that what is learned will be a solid foundation for the next phase.

3.2.8. Suggested Outline of Grammar Topics by Grades

Grammar Topic	4th	5th	6th	7th	8th
1= introduction; 2= practice & application; 3 review & mastery					
Parts of the Sentence					
Article	3	3	3	3	3
Gender	1	1	3	3	3
Number	1	2	3	3	3
Formation and use of contractions: al. del		1	2	3	3
Nouns:					
Gender of nouns	1	2	3	3	3
Number (singular and plural)	1	2	3	3	3
Agreement in gender and number with articles	1	2	3	3	3
Adjectives					
Adjectives of quality	1	2	3	3	3
Demonstrative adjectives		1	2	3	3
Possessive adjectives	1	2	3	3	3
Numbers	1	2	3	3	3
Comparatives and superlatives			1	2	3
Shortened form of some adjectives (gran. grande)	1	2	3	3	3
Agreement in gender and number with article and noun	1	2	3	3	3
Position of adjectives		1	2	3	3
Pronouns					
Personal	2	3	3	3	3
Reflexive	1	2	3	3	3
Direct object				2	3
Indirect object				2	3
Prepositional pronouns				1	2
Verbs					
Regular, present tense	2	3	3	3	3
Regular, simple past tense			1	2	3
Regular, imperfect tense			1	3	3
Comparing uses of the above tenses				1	2
Future tense, "ir a" + infinitive				1	2
Irregular, present: **ser, tener,** and the **gustar** construction	1	2	3	3	3

	1	2	3	4	5
Estar	1	2	3	3	3
Ser y estar		2	3	3	3
Querer, poder, ir, hacer		1	2	3	3
Decir, saber, conocer, dar, salir		1	2	3	3
Jugar, volver, dormir, preferir, empezar, traer, venir, etc.			1	2	3
Irregular verbs in past tenses				1	2
Progressive			1	2	3
Perfect tenses (present perfect)					1
Imperative				1	2
Conditional: gustar		1	2	3	3
Conjunctions	1	2	3	3	3
Prepositions	2	3	3	3	3
Adverbs					
Of place	2	3	3	3	3
Of time	2	2	3	3	3
Of means			1	2	3
Of quantity	1	2	3	3	3
Of negation and affirmation		1	2	3	3
Shortening of certain adverbs	1	2	3	3	3
Adverbial phrases		1	2	3	3
Interrogatives					
Qué, cómo, cuándo, dónde, adónde, cuánto, quién, quiénes, cuál, cuáles, por qué	1	2	3	3	3

Chapter 4

Poetry, Dramatization, and Recitation

Introduction

"With poetry a person creates, reveals his inner being, which is received by the deepest inner being of another human being when the latter absorbs the created work."

– Rudolf Steiner

We have previously explained the importance of speech and recitation in Waldorf schools, exploring how the child enters into the soul of another culture through poetry, either by means of folk sentiment or the expression of poetic lyricism. With regard to the pedagogical value of poetry, Dr. Heinz Zimmermann tells us that, to strengthen our speech ability, we have to be in active connection with what we call the spirit of the language. There are several ways of doing it. One is to dedicate ourselves intensely to the lyrical poetry, which teaches us about the value of the different language parts.

When she is about to teach poetry, the teacher has to live with the chosen poem before entering the classroom, and memorize it in its totality; she has to have a clear image of what she is going to recite. In this way the poetry takes on a living quality, in which the images will not only live in the class, but also will reverberate in the air, bringing poetry to an experiential level, not just a merely auditory one.

A lengthy poem, especially in the early grades, is not an impediment, since the acquisitive powers of imitation are at their peak. In these grades it is important to choose rhythmical poems in which rhyme predominates, since musicality is essential when students are learning a language. René Querido tells us that musicality and temperament are emphasized in the recitation of the poem. Of course, the teacher chooses poetry of excellent quality. A rich repertoire of poetry is created, which is learned by heart, through oral practice. This is an invaluable treasure for the rest of the students' lives.

Once the teacher has the poem memorized, she should study how to present it. In the early grades she should try out gestures, movements, and intonation that will accompany the recitation. Also, she should plan activities that help the children create an image of what is being said. In the upper grades, the teacher will have to formulate a brief story as an introduction to the poem, and plan the presentation of the key vocabulary.

Let us now look at examples from first grade to eighth, which illustrate methods that can be used for teaching poetry.

First Grade

"A MARGARITA DEBAYLE"
by Rubén Darío

Margarita, está linda la mar
y el viento
lleva esencia sutil de azahar;
yo siento
en el alma una alondra cantar,
tu acento.
Margarita te voy a contar
un cuento.
Este era un rey que tenía
un palacio de diamantes,
una tienda hecha del día
y un rebaño de elefantes,
un kiosko de malaquita,
un gran manto de tisú,
y una gentil princesita,
tan bonita,
Margarita,
tan bonita como tú.
Una tarde la princesa
vio una estrella aparecer;
la princesa era traviesa
y la quiso ir a coger.
La quería para hacerla
decorar un prendador,
con un verso y una perla,
una pluma y una flor.

Las princesas primorosas
se parecen mucho a ti:
cortan lirios, cortan rosas,
cortan astros. Son así.

Pues se fue la niña bella
bajo el cielo y sobre el mar,
a cortar la blanca estrella
que la hacía suspirar.

Y siguió camino arriba,
por la luna y más allá;
mas lo malo es que ella iba
sin permiso de papá.

Cuando estuvo ya de vuelta
de los parques del Señor,
se miraba toda envuelta
en un suave resplandor.
Y el rey dijo: "¿Qué te has hecho?
te he buscado y no te hallé;
y ¿qué tienes en el pecho,
que encendido se te ve?"
La princesa no mentía.
Y así dijo la verdad:
"Fui a cortar la estrella mía
a la azul inmensidad".
Y el rey clama: "¿No te he dicho
que el azul no has de tocar?
¡Qué locura! ¡Qué capricho!
El Señor se va a enojar".
Y dice ella: "No hubo intento;
yo me fui no sé por qué;
por las olas, por el viento
fui a la estrella y la corté":
Y el papá dice enojado:
"Un castigo has de tener:
vuelve al cielo, y lo robado
vas ahora a devolver".
La princesa se entristece
por la dulce flor de luz,
cuando entonces aparece
sonriendo el buen Jesús.

Y así dice: "En mis campiñas
esa rosa le ofrecí:
son mis flores de las niñas
que al soñar piensan en mí".

Viste el rey ropas brillantes,
y luego hace desfilar
cuatrocientos elefantes
a las orillas de la mar.

La princesa está bella,
pues ya tiene el prendedor,
el que luce con la estrella,
verso, perla, pluma y flor.

Margarita, está linda la mar
y el viento lleva esencia sutil de azahar:
tu aliento.
Ya que lejos de mí vas a estar
guarda, niña, un gentil pensamiento
al que un día te quiso contar
un cuento.

It might take six months or more for the children to learn this poem. Harmonious movements should be added to express what one is saying, which will be imitated by the students. On the first day, everyone stands in silence. The teacher recites each verse, the students repeat, and then everybody repeats again together. We go on to the next verse and do the same thing, until we get to the end of the stanza being presented. Then we do a recapitulation of the stanza from the beginning, everyone repeating together. The poem should be repeated every day at the start of class, for several minutes, adding verses according to the progress of the students. The key to learning is regular repetition. With this poem some teachers omit the first stanza, since they want the students who are going to dramatize it to be the protagonists, instead of Margarita. Therefore, they begin with the stanza that describes the king: "Este era un rey que…"

At the end of several weeks, when they have learned two or more stanzas, it is possible to bring to class costumes or symbolical elements, such as a king's cape, a princess' cape, a large cardboard star, a blue veil to represent the water of the sea, and a light blue veil representing the sky, and elephant masks. This will help the students to get excited and carry out the learning in an artistic manner.

The dramatization will be carried out in the second phase of the class, and the students will be seated. If the teacher lacks space for the dramatization, it is necessary to ask the students to move their desks and create the necessary space. Then the roles are assigned. The king, the princess, the star, two volunteers for the sea and the sky, and some elephants. We can incorporate into the dramatization a few instruments like a drum, a xylophone, or a lyre, which will underscore musically certain moments of the play. Then, begin!

The focus is on recitation, on the development of movements, and on acting out the play let. All the students will begin with the recitation; at the right moment the king comes out, and the princess arrives. The king enters and points to his possessions:

> Este era un rey que tenía
> Un palacio de diamantes…

The king disappears from the scene. The princess moves freely about looking at the horizon, and sees a star in the distance. The class continues the recitation:

> Una tarde la princesa
> Vio una estrella aparecer…

Xylophone music. The princess appears moving among the veils, which will be moved by two children, giving the effect of the sky. Others, with eurythmy movements, can be the wind. Then two children appear, moving a long, blue veil across the scene. A rain stick can give the effect of rain, while the princess walks on the waves of the sea. We recite:

> Las princesas primorosas
> Se parecen mucho a ti…

The princess cuts the star and returns to the palace, walking on the sea, holding by the hand a girl who will carry a large star of cardboard. The king is waiting for her. When they arrive, the star will be placed toward the rear but is still visible. The king looks angry. The whole class recites chorally, while the actors move:

> Cuando estuvo ya de vuelta
> de los parques del Señor…

The king disappears from the scene with an angry gesture. The princess weeps to lyre or xylophone music. In the distance an angel appears and brings a star in his hand. Everyone recites:

> La princesa se entristece
> por la dulce flor de luz…

The angel gives the star to the princess and disappears from the scene. The king, waiting for the right moment, enters with a herd of elephants. Drums sound. We recite:

> Viste el Rey ropas brillantes,
> y luego hace desfilar…

We end the play in a semicircle singing a song that goes with the story, which perhaps the music teacher could compose.

It must be kept in mind that when poetry recitation is carried out in the rhythmical phase of the lesson, it is going to be only one segment integrated into a repertoire of recitation. This means that the greetings, songs, movements, and recitations are progressively presented and are going to occupy several minutes. It should be understood that this repertory is spoken daily in the language classes, and new songs and other elements will be gradually incorporated.

Even though the recitation of the poem is done as an integral part of class, the costumes and props should be used only occasionally. They should not be exploited for the sake of avoiding boredom. Other activities could include drawing some of the scenes.

Second Grade

As mentioned earlier, second grade is the year of fables. Many are in rhymed verse and are very easy to recite and dramatize. An example is *El burro flautista* by Tomás Irirarte.

> Esta fabulilla,
> salga bien o salga mal,
> me ha ocurrido
> por casualidad.
> Cerca de unos prados
> que hay en mi lugar
> pasaba un borrico
> por casualidad.
> Una flauta en ellos
> halló, que un zagal
> se dejó olvidada
> por casualidad.
> Acercóse a olerla
> el dicho animal;
> y dio un resoplido
> por casualidad.
> En la flauta el aire
> se hubo de colar;
> y sonó la flauta
> por casualidad.
> —¡Oh –dijo el borrico—,
> ¡qué bien sé tocar!
> Y dirán que es mala
> La música asnal.
> Sin reglas del arte
> borriquitos hay
> que una vez aciertan
> por casualidad.

Just as in first grade, the fable should recited daily. This fable is relatively brief, and the students can learn it in a short time; a few weeks later, costumes can be added: some goat masks, a donkey mask, a shepherd's hat, and a recorder.

The scene begins with the shepherd boy herding the goats through the meadow (background music can be played). The shepherd, seated in the meadow, begins to play his pentatonic flute. When he finishes, "deja olvidada la flauta en el prado," the donkey enters and the recitation begins while the donkey acts. Upon finishing, we can conclude with the song "Burrito Pepe," adding humor and sympathy to our know-it-all donkey.

Third Grade

"El Molino"
By A. Fernández Grillo

Sigue el agua su camino
y al pasar por la arboleda
mueve impaciente la rueda
del solitario molino.
Cantan alegres
los molineros
llevando el trigo
de los graneros;
trémula el agua
lenta camina;
rueda la rueda,
brota la harina
y allá en el fondo
del caserío
al par del hombre
trabaja el río.
La campesina tarea
cesa con el sol poniente,
y la luna solamente
guarda la paz de la aldea.

At this age the imitative powers of the children are diminishing, since now they are beginning to acquire a sense of their own individuality. This is the time when the teacher needs a strong presence and meaningful gestures to impart life to the poem.

Little by little the pupils will create gestures rather imitate the teacher. Gesture now begins to be an extension of speech. Daily practice is essential, as in previous years. After the choral recitation, the teacher can present an illustration that describes the poem. This will help them to project a mental image of what is being said, as a memory aid, and to begin acquiring and relating to the vocabulary of the poem. On presenting the illustration, we can work on the vocabulary. Example: with the illustration of a mill, we can ask questions such as:

¿Dónde está el Molino? ¿Tiene una rueda el molino? ¿Por dónde pasa el agua?

At this age it is also necessary to give them a challenge. When they are seated expectantly, we can then ask a volunteer to come to the front of the class and recite part or all of the poem without help. When the poem has been learned, we can pass on to the dramatization if the teacher so wishes. Among the volunteers, some can be the mills, others are wheels, millers, trees and water. The student, since he knows the poem by heart, feels quite comfortable. This is why we can let them act out the poem and express themselves freely with gestures.

During third grade it is important to introduce tongue twisters, which help enunciation and vocalization of the sounds. The challenge of learning these tongue twisters well suits the child at this age.

Fourth Grade

Recitation in this year is powerful, repetitive, and if possible should have a lot of alliteration. An example is *Estando la mora en su lugar*.

From now on it is quite clear that recitation will be done with less movement, but with small gestures that arise from the need to express oneself. This does not mean that the teacher should not study the best gestures to illustrate what is being recited, inasmuch as the gestures help the student to remember the recitation. However, students many times are going to gesture freely, and other times perhaps are going to imitate.

As in previous years, daily recitation begins each lesson. After two or three lessons we can bring to the class illustrations of a fly, a blackberry, a spider, a rat, and all the other characters of the poem. The student already knows many of these animals from earlier Spanish grades, and now asks himself what is going on in the poem that is being recited.

The presentation of the poem can be carried out in several ways: distributing the drawings and reciting in segments by turns, while showing the drawings; using masks, in which case the actors will stay out of view of the public and will enter in accord with the recitation; letting the student choose the character he wants to play and he himself creates, by means of a drawing, an original mask or costume (not commercial); or, finally, it could be presented in the form of choral poetry, with the characters coming out in turn, moving to the events of the poem.

The music teacher can be invited to cooperate in the presentation, playing an instrument to add more interest, wit, and humor.

"ESTANDO LA MORA EN SU LUGAR"

Estando la mora en su lugar,
vino la mosca y le hizo mal:
La mosca a la mora,
en su moralito sola…
Estando la mosca en su lugar,
Vino la araña y le hizo mal:
La araña a la mosca,
la mosca a la mora,
en su moralito sola…
Estando la araña en su lugar,
vino la rata y le hizo mal:
La rata a la araña,
la araña a la mosca,
la mosca a la mora,
en su moralito sola…
Estando la rata en su lugar,
vino el gato y le hizo mal:
El gato a la rata,
la rata a la araña,
la araña a la mosca,
la mosca a la mora,
en su moralito sola…
Estando el gato en su lugar,
vino el perro y le hizo mal:
el perro al gato,
el gato a la rata,
la rata a la araña,
la araña a la mosca,
la mosca a la mora,
en su moralito sola…
Estando el perro en su lugar,
vino el palo y le hizo mal:
el palo al perro,
el perro al gato,
el gato a la rata,
la rata a la araña,
la araña a la mosca,
la mosca a la mora,
en su moralito sola…

Estando el palo en su lugar,
vino el fuego y le hizo mal:
el fuego al palo,
el palo al perro,
el perro al gato,
el gato a la rata,
la rata a la araña,
la araña a la mosca,
la mosca a la mora,
en su moralito sola…
Estando el fuego en su lugar,
vino el agua y le hizo mal:
el agua al fuego,
el fuego al palo,
el palo al perro,
el perro al gato,
el gato a la rata,
la rata a la araña,
la araña a la mosca,
la mosca a la mora,
en su moralito sola…
Estando el agua en su lugar,
vino la vaca y le hizo mal:
la vaca al agua,
el agua al fuego,
el fuego al palo,
el palo al perro,
el perro al gato,
el gato a la rata,
la rata a la araña,
la araña a la mosca,
la mosca a la mora,
en su moralito sola…
Estando la vaca en su lugar,
vino el toro y le hizo mal:
el toro a la vaca,
la vaca al agua,
el agua al fuego,
el fuego al palo,
el palo al perro,
el perro al gato,
el gato a la rata,
la rata a la araña,
la araña a la mosca,

la mosca a la mora,
en su moralito sola...

In fourth grade, a popular work about the Aztecs can be dramatized because notions of physical strength, power, and resistance are beginning to develop in the fourth—and fifth grader as well. To these can be added other important traits, such as individuality, freedom, and a great interest and curiosity about earthly materials. The power of redemption arises with the hope of culminating in a new life.

This drama project can be realized in the fifth grade. The work, titled *Los aztecas*, unfolds in the following manner:

To the beat of drums, the Aztec kings appear on stage, dancing energetically in a row, with scepters held aloft with both hands, and singing "Conish," a song dedicated to corn. Then they form a semicircle, leaning their scepters on the floor. Next, four students approach the audience and begin to dance, always to the beat of the drums, in a simple melody where they show the strength and coordination of movements of an Aztec dancer. Immediately, two students who play the role of Spanish historians, dressed in black clothing, capes, boots and Spanish hat, read from a document what each king will later relate. The reading is done in English so that the audience can understand what is being said. Having finished their stories, the kings place their scepters on the floor, join their hands, and recite the poem *Himno entre ruinas*. They end the play marching at first and then they begin to sing and dance while they exit the stage.

The Aztec Kings and Their Works

Historian: history tells us the life of each of these kings. Each king will tell what he did.

1. Acamapichtli: Yo soy el primer rey Acamapichtli que quiere decir "El que Empuña el Cetro." Después de una larga y penosa vida errante, mi pueblo me nombró su rey. Mi pueblo y yo fundamos la gran ciudad de Tenochtitlán.

2. Huitzilihuitl: "Pájaro de Rico Plumaje" quiere decir Huitzilihuitl. Yo soy el segundo rey. Mi pueblo edificó las primeras casas de piedra y comenzaron a usar los primeros trajes de tela de algodón.

3. Chimalpopoca: Yo soy el tercer rey y mí nombre Chimalpopoca quiere decir "El Escudo que Humea". Mi pueblo, con gran esfuerzo, logró el uso del agua en sus hogares.

4   Izxoatl: Yo soy el cuarto rey y mi nombre quiere decir "Serpientes de Navajas". Tuve la gran oportunidad de salvar a mi pueblo del feroz Maxtla. Con la ayuda de Netzahualcóyotl conseguimos la independencia de mi pueblo.

5   Moctezuma Primero: Yo soy el quinto rey. Mi nombre quiere decir "Flechador del Cielo". Fui muy valiente. Mi pueblo construyó un dique de piedra para evitar inundaciones. Fui el creador del Imperio Azteca. Empañé mi gloria con un fanatismo religioso.

6   Atzayácatl: "Cara de Agua" quiere decir mi nombre Atzayácatl. Yo soy el sexto rey. Fui guerrero como mis antepasados. Conseguí varias conquistas para expandir el territorio de Tenochtitlán.

7   Tizoc: Me llamo Tizoc y yo soy el séptimo rey. Mi nombre está representado por un jeroglífico en forma de una piedra tiznada; por eso me llaman "El Tiznado". Mandé construir el templo mayor. Fomenté la idolatría.

8   Ahuizotl: Yo soy el octavo rey. Me llamo Ahuizotl, nombre que está representado por un animal anfibio que puede vivir en la tierra y en el agua. Fui muy valiente y mi territorio se extendió hasta Chiapas y Guatemala.

9   Moctezuma Xocoyotzin Segundo: Me llamo Moctezuma Xocoyotzin y yo soy el noveno rey. Mi nombre quiere decir "El Señor valeroso más joven". Durante mi reinado, llegaron los hombres blancos, los españoles. Fui emperador y sumo sacerdote de carácter altivo, severo y supersticioso. Fui déspota con los humildes y servil con los extranjeros. Creí que los españoles eran dioses.

10 Cuitláhuac: Yo soy el décimo rey y me llamo Cuitláhuac. Fui hermano de Moctezuma Segundo pero fui distinto a él. Mi nombre quiere decir "Tierra Seca". Mi pueblo y yo derrotamos al conquistador Hernán Cortés. Contraje la enfermedad de la viruela traída por los españoles.

11 Tenochtli: Yo soy el undécimo rey. Mi nombre, Tenochtli, quiere decir "Tuna hecha de piedra". Durante mi reinado, fue hecha una ceremonia por el fuego nuevo.

12 Cuauhtémoc: Me llamo Cuauhtémoc que quiere decir "Águila que baja". Yo soy el duodécimo rey. Subí al trono al desaparecer el imperio azteca. Fui leal a los principios de mi amada tierra y por eso me quemaron los pies. Fui también el último rey.

Everyone: (they hold hands and raise their arms) Esperamos que la historia nos haya enseñado a tomar las buenas cualidades de estos reyes. (Then they recite "Himno entre ruinas").

"Himno Entre Ruinas"

by Octavio Paz

Día, redondo día,
luminosa naranja
de veinticuatro gajos,
todos atravesados
por una misma y amarilla dulzura,
la inteligencia en fin se encarna en forma,
se reconcilian las dos mitades enemigas,
la conciencia-espejo se licúa
vuelve a ser fuente,
manantial de fábulas,
hombre, árbol de imágenes,
palabras que son flores,
que son frutos,
que son actos.

*An example of the clothes of an Aztec king
drawn by a sixth-grade Waldorf student.*

102

HIMNO ENTRE RUINAS

(Octavio Paz)

Día, redondo día,
luminosa naranja
de venticuatro gajos,
todos atravesados
por una misma y amarilla dulzura,
la inteligencia en fin se encarna en forma,
se reconcilian las dos mitades enemigas,
la conciencia-espejo se licúa
vuelve a ser fuente,
manantial de fábulas,
hombre, árrbol de imágenes,
palabras que son flores,
que son frutos,
que son actos.

Fifth Grade

Three examples: "Mariposa del aire" by Federico García Lorca
"Plantemos el árbol" by Enrique E. Rivarola
"Leyenda incaica de Manco Capac and Mama
Ocllo"
"Mariposa del aire" can be worked on with the eurythmy teacher.
This poem allows us to explore movements and spatial dimensions that
are quite appropriate for the age of the pupils.

"Mariposa del aire"
by Federico García Lorca

Mariposa del aire,
¡Qué hermosa eres!
mariposa del aire,
dorada y verde,
luz del candil,
mariposa del aire
¡Quédate ahí, ahí, ahí…!
No te quieres parar,
pararte no quieres,
mariposa del aire,
dorada y verde,
luz del candil,
mariposa del aire,
¡Quédate ahí, ahí, ahí…!
¡Quédate ahí!
Mariposa, ¿estás ahí?

"Plantemos el árbol"
by Enrique E. Rivarola

Abramos la tierra, plantemos el árbol,
será nuestro amigo y aquí crecerá,
y un día vendremos buscando su abrigo,
y flores y frutas y sombra dará.

El cielo benigno dé riego a su planta,
el sol de septiembre le dé su calor,
la tierra su jugo dará a sus raíces,
y tengan sus hojas verdura y frescor.

Plantemos el árbol, el árbol amigo,
sus ramas frondosas aquí extenderá,
y un día vendremos buscando sus flores
y sombra y fruta y flores dará.

"Plantemos el árbol" can be done in the following way:

At the beginning, in the first two weeks, the whole class works on the poem, repeating it after the teacher. The teacher presents it with gestures that he has worked out, giving an idea of what we are reciting. The third week the class is divided into two groups, and each group will be in charge of different parts of the poem.

Inca legend: Manco Capac y Mama Ocllo

Like other advanced civilizations, the Incas have an extensive history. Therefore we need to limit ourselves to dramatizing the famous legend of the first kings, Manco Capac and his wife, Mama Ocllo. The outcome of this story perhaps led to the goal of attaining good social organization.

What is more, one can say that the Incas' civilization flowed from a spirit of virtues, from a light inspired by forces of love. The connection of the sun and the moon was extensively studied in the Egyptian culture as well. The hypothesis was reached that the sun manifests as the supreme god who desires harmony among his children. The Egyptian myth of Osiris, Isis and Horus versus that of Manco Capac, Mama Ocllo leads us to believe that, despite the distances, and different epochs and languages, the stories could be indirectly linked. The mummies, rafts of bulrushes, papyrus, and exceptional skill in the arts accentuate the similarities.

The play

In a procession, the peasants enter first, then the king and queen, and finally, the Sun God. The music of "El Cóndor Pasa" accompanies the procession. Half the peasants go to one side of the stage, and the other half to the other side. The king and queen go to the center, and the Sun God goes to a higher place.

Un campesino:
(Stands in the center of the stage and shouts in Quechua language:)

DO NOT STEAL, DO NOT LIE, DO NOT BE LAZY

AMASÚA (all repeat this word aloud)
AMALLULLA (all repeat this word aloud)

AMAQUELLA (all repeat this word aloud)

Coro 1:   El Dios Sol, según la leyenda, veía desde lo alto como
            la gente se exterminaba y la Tierra estaba llena de odio.
            (Six students fight with sticks. Sun God standing on a
            high spot, shakes his head and looks sad).

Coro 2:   Se compadeció de esos hombres y decidió que era
            preciso enseñarles a vivir en paz y en forma civilizada.
            (Manco Capac and Mama Ocllo appear onstage.)

Dios Sol: Tú, Manco Capac, y tú, Mama Ocllo, serán guías y
            maestros de sus hijos.

M.C. y M.O.: (They answer kneeling) Así lo haremos, Dios Sol.

Dios Sol: (Continues speaking to Manco Capac and Mama Ocllo)
            Con esta varita de oro vayan tocando el suelo. Donde se
            hunda, allí fundarán la capital del Imperio.

M.C. y M.O.: Sí, Dios Sol.

Coro 3:   (Two students represent Lake Titicaca with blue cloths.
            The rest of the class is working, fighting, or arguing)
            Manco Capac y Mama Ocllo se aparecieron a los
            hombres entre las espumas del lago Titicaca.

M.C. y M.O.: Sean buenos y vivirán felices como el Dios Sol lo
            desea. Les enseñaremos muchas obras para progresar,
            pero nos tienen que seguir.
            Los campesinos (They look at each other)
            Vamos con ellos. Sí, sí, vamos con ellos.

M.C. y M.O.: (peasants doing different activities but always fighting
            while Manco Capac and Mama Ocllo walk from one
            side to the other persuading them to follow them.)
            Vengan con nosotros. Les enseñaremos muchas cosas
            para su progreso.
            (Many peasants follow them)

Coro 4:   Caminaron muchos días tocando el suelo con la varita.
            Un día, finalmente, llegaron al cerro de Huanacaure, en
            el valle del Cuzco, y Manco Capac tanteó ahí con la

Campesinos: varita y ¡y ésta se hundió!

 ¡Encontramos el lugar prometido! ¡Alabado sea el Dios Sol! ¡Alabado sea Manco Capac y su esposa, Mama Ocllo!

 (After this praise, the peasants, to the rhythm of the bass drum and the"chajchas," all sing the song "El Sairirí," with the exception of the Sun God)

M.C.: (kneeling) Dios Sol, Manco Capac me has llamado, por ser tu hijo y de la Luna. Seré merecedor de mi nombre, Todo Poderoso. Enseñaré a unificar los pueblos y vivir en armonía.

M.O.: Con honor seré la compañera de Manco Capac. Enseñaré a las mujeres a hilar y tejer y también a adorarte a ti, Dios Sol, y a nuestra madre Luna.

Dios Sol: Buen trabajo han hecho, mis hijos. Sigan siendo buenos guías y maestros de sus futuros hijos.

All, except the king and queen and Sun God:

 Pasaron muchos años y esta raza se convirtió en una raza tranquila y mística, siendo grandes proveedores del sustento de cada uno de sus habitantes y con muchos dones artísticos y científicos.

(This play ends with a very active dance called "El Humahuaqueño," better known as "El carnavalito." Then all leave in a procession to the rhythm of the music, "El Cóndor Pasa," first the peasants, then the "ñusta"—the girl devoted to the Sun God, throwing flowers before the path of the king and queen, who then exit—and finally the Sun God).

"El Sairirí del Ande"
(Andean song for the Inca legend)

Tengo que llegar al pueblo
allí me espera mi madre
tierra de gente morena
paisaje color ahuayo
tierra de gente morena
paisaje color ahuayo
Soy el Sairirí del Ande
caminando muchas lunas
con el huairaje andino

envuelto en mil colores
con el valor de mi raza
echando ponchos al viento.
("Sairirí" means travelling musician or Andean troubador)

El Humahuaqueo (andean-huayño song)

Llegando está el carnaval
quebradeño mi cholita
llegando está el carnaval
quebradeño mi cholita
Fiesta de la quebrada
humahuaqueña para bailar
erke, charango, y bombo
carnavalito para gozar.

Quebradeño, humahuaqueñito,
quebradeño, humahuaqueñito
Fiesta de la quebrada
humahuaqueña para bailar
erke, charango, y bombo
carnavalito para gozar.
Lai, lai, lai, lara, la, ra…
Fiesta de la quebrada
humahuaqueña para bailar
erke, charango, y bombo
carnavalito para gozar.

*Drawing by a sixth-grade student from
the Waldorf School of the Peninsula.*

Sixth Grade

From sixth grade on, the student is prepared to work with more complex poems and other works. Below is an example of such a poem.

"La muralla" by Nicolás Guillén

Step 1. Preparation: As we pointed out earlier, the teacher has to memorize the poem entirely and recite it with expressiveness.

Step 2. Presentation of the vocabulary: The key vocabulary should be taught before introducing the poem. Depending on the class, this could take between one and four classes. The new words should be presented artistically and in context, not in isolation. For instance, to introduce "muralla" we could use images of the Great Wall of China and of a stone-wall. Then we can invite the students to describe walls, compare them, and speak about their functions. Why do people build walls?

Step 3. Conceptualization of the poem: Once the class is familiar with the vocabulary, the teacher tells them that a poet imagined being able to build a wall across the island to leave outside the things he didn't like and let in only the people and the things he liked. The class is divided into groups of four to six students and asked to make a sketch of the island with a wall in the middle ("desde la playa hasta el monte, desde el monte hasta la playa"). Then they have to write or draw on one side of the wall the things that they would like to have on their side, and on the other side the things that they wouldn't allow in. After 10 or 15 minutes, they present their ideas to the class. (If appropriate, this is an excellent opportunity to practice the future and the conditional tenses).

Step 4. Learning the poem: Now they are ready to listen to the poem and listen to the choices the poet has made. The teacher recites it for them and asks them to identify some of the things that they heard. Then they should repeat the poem following the teacher. Together they make two lists on the board with the headings Yes and No, and they write all the items mentioned by the author: "una rosa y un clavel, el sable del coronel," etc. Each student is assigned an element to draw on a card.

In the next class, the teacher writes the first stanza on the board. The cards are collected and placed on the border of the blackboard. Then the poem is recited, paying attention to the intonation and expression. It is important to incorporate these qualities from the beginning. As they begin to feel more comfortable with the first stanza, the section with "Tun, Tun" is added, using the cards as an aid instead of the written words.

Now the poem is familiar, and they are ready to memorize it. Some words are erased from the board, and the poem is read again. Then more words are erased while the recitation is repeated, until they reach their limits or until all of the words are erased. It is important to leave the first word of each line until the end. The students should read the poem before going to bed and upon arising.

In the next class we review what has already been practiced and continue with the rest of the poem. Cards are used as a memory aid for the section that begins with "Al corazón del amigo" and the last stanza is written on the board; we carefully observe the differences between this stanza and the first one.

Now they are ready to practice it by interpreting it in a variety of forms. Half the class can say "Tun, tun" while the other group says "¿Quién es?" Each card can be handed to a pair of students. The students then form a wall; some can act as a door that opens and closes. This is an excellent poem for assemblies and presentations to the community.

La muralla
By Nicolás Guillén

Para hacer esta muralla,
tráiganme todas las manos:
los negros, sus manos negras,
los blancos, sus manos blancas.

Ay,
Una muralla que vaya
desde la playa hasta el monte,
desde la playa hasta el monte, bien
allá sobre el horizonte.
—¡Tun, tun!
—¿Quién es?
—Una rosa y un clavel…
—¡Abre la muralla!

—¡Tun, tun!
—¿Quién es?
—El sable del coronel…
—¡Cierra la muralla!

—¡Tun, tun!
—¿Quién es
—La paloma y el laurel…
—¡Abre la muralla!

—¡Tun, tun!
—¿Quién es?
—El alacrán y el ciempiés…
—¡Cierra la muralla!

Al corazón de un amigo,
abre la muralla,
al veneno y al puñal,
cierra la muralla,
al mirto y la yerbabuena,
abre la muralla;
al diente de la serpiente,
cierra la muralla;
al ruiseñor en la flor,
abre la muralla…

Alcemos una muralla,
Juntando todas las manos
los negros, sus manos negras,
los blancos, sus manos blancas.

Unas muralla que vaya
Desde la playa hasta el monte,

Desde el monte hasta la playa, bien
allá sobre el horizonte…

Given the new individuality that the students acquire in this grade, the time arrives to make the recitations more individual. The students need more than ever to have a mental image of what they are repeating, especially when they recite sections of a poem.

Epic ballads and descriptive poetry are the predominant types appropriate for this age. The repetition found in some old ballads will facilitate learning them, either in groups or by individuals.

The Spanish "romance" or ballad is derived in its earliest versions from the epic poems that were spread in the Middle Ages by minstrels. The *Romancero español*, an extensive collection of Spanish ballads, is a very appropriate form for class, for its historic content and its epic style. These old ballads relate the stories of the heroes of that period, for instance, El Cid, long considered Spain's national hero.

Another play that we have chosen is the *Auto de Reyes Magos*, a thirteenth century work, and its adaptation for children by Eugenio Florit. Another version of this play, together with *Paradise* and *The Shepherds,* form a trilogy of Christmas plays produced in many Waldorf schools during Christmas and Epiphany. Steiner recovered the latter plays during one of his visits to the Austrian countryside. They are plays that the country folk of Austria have relived with enthusiasm and simplicity year after year and by oral tradition since remote times.

Los Reyes Magos (The Three Wise Kings) is the oldest verse play known in Spanish, and is one of the most important works from medieval times. Only some parts have been preserved. They are ingenuous and beautiful, relating the encounter of the Wise Men, the following of the star, and the visit with Herod.

These plays' sense of hope and renewal capture the essence of Christmas. *The Shepherds* and *La Posada* (Mexican Christmas ceremony) likewise both have their origin in religious theater, which was represented in the churches of the Middle Ages.

Let's look at an example of the play *Los Reyes Magos*.

The students selected to play the roles of Melchor, Gaspar, Baltasar, and Herod will have to memorize their lines during Christmas vacation. Before that, they have had to practice individually during recess. The angel will practice with the music teacher the solo that he or she will sing.

The play can begin with the song "Los tres reyes magos," Spanish version by J.H. Hopkins of "We Three Kings or Orient Are," or a popular song about the Three Wise Kings, such as the one given by Lulú Delacre in her book *Las navidades en Latinoamérica*.

Escena 1

All the actors walk toward center stage from opposite angles. As they sing, they approach the stage in order. The lyrics of the song are as follows:

> Los tres reyes, henos aquí.
> Lejos nuestra patria está.
> Siempre fuimos y seguimos la estrella que nos guió.
> Oh, oh, astro lleno de amor,
> de belleza y fulgor,
> tu camino nos conduce
> al eterno esplendor.

The actors enter the stage and sit down on benches at the sides, remaining still, as in the representations of the Middle Ages. Herod's court is on one side; on the other, the shepherds and the manger scene.

The Wise Kings approach from different parts of the stage. Gaspar speaks while holding his telescope. Then Baltasar, followed by Melchor, without any contact between them. The three watch the star from different roads. Each king is dressed in a color: red, green, and blue.

Gaspar (alone):
> Dios creador ¡qué maravilla!
> ¿Cuál es la estrella que así brilla?

La veo allí por vez primera
como si ahora mismo naciera.
¿Nacido el creador
que de las gentes es señor?
No es cierto; caso tan extraño
no puede ser más que engaño.
Otra noche la miraré
y si es verdad, bien lo sabré. (pause)
mas, ¿por qué no ha de ser cierto
lo que en los cielos hoy advierto?
(pause)

La señal no puede ser
sino la que hoy se deja ver.
Nacido es Dios, de hembra nacido
en este mes amortecido.
Allá iré, lo adoraré,
por Dios de todos lo tendré

Baltasar enters from another side alone, carrying his telescope:

Esta estrella no sé dónde viene,
ni quién la trae ni quién la tiene.
¿Por qué será esta señal?
En mis días no vi tal.
cierto, nacido ha en la tierra
aquel que en paz o en guerra
Señor ha de ser de Oriente
lo mismo que del Occidente.
Por tres noches la miraré
y más de veras lo sabré. (pause)
No hay duda, Dios es ya nacido
que yo lo tengo bien entendido.
Iré, le adoraré
y honraré y rogaré.

Melchor exits and speaks to himself as he looks at the heavens with his telescope:

Valga el Creador- que no fue hallada
ni en escrituras encontrada-.
tal estrella no estaba en el cielo,
de esto soy yo buen estrellero.
bien ahora lo puedo ver

que un hombre ha nacido de mujer,
que es Señor de toda la tierra
y lo que el cielo en él encierra;
de todas las gentes Señor;
bien lo veo que es verdad.
Allá iré, por caridad.

Escena II

Gaspar and Baltasar meet and speak to each other:

Gaspar:

Dios os salve, señor; ¿sois buen estrellero?
Decidme la verdad, de vos saberla quiero.
¿Visteis jamás tal maravilla?
¿La estrella que en el cielo brilla?

Baltasar:

Nacido es el creador
que de las gentes es Señor.
Iré, le adoraré.

Gaspar:

También yo le rogaré.

Escena III

(Melchor enters and meets the other two kings on stage).
Melchor:

Señores, ¿a qué tierra queréis andar?
¿Queréis ir conmigo al creador honrar?
¿También lo habéis visto? Yo lo voy a adorar.

Gaspar:

Veamos por ventura si le podremos hallar.
Vayamos tras la estrella, veremos el lugar.

Melchor:

¿Y cómo comprobaremos si es hombre mortal,
o si es rey de la tierra, o si es rey celestial?

Baltasar:

¿Queréis saber cómo lo entenderemos?
Oro, mirra e incienso a él ofreceremos.

Si fuere rey de tierra, el oro lo querrá,
Si fuese hombre mortal, la mirra tomará,
Y si es Rey celestial, estos dos dejará,
Tomará el incienso que le pertenecerá.
Gaspar y Melchor together:
Andemos, pues, y así lo haremos,
Nuestros dones le ofreceremos.

Escena IV

(The kings move toward the court of King Herod, which to now has been immobile, on the left side of the stage. Herod appears seated on a throne with his court. The kings walk as they sing the song of "Los tres Reyes Magos." Finally the three kings address Herod and speak:)

Melchor:

Sávete el creador, Dios te guarde de mal.

Gaspar:

Dios dé larga vida y te guarde de mal.

Baltasar:

Vamos en romería a aquel Rey adorar,
que ha nacido en la tierra y no podemos hallar.

Herodes:

¿Qué decís? ¿dónde vais? ¿a quién vais a buscar?
¿De qué tierra venís, ¿dónde queréis andar?
Decidme vuestros nombres, no los queráis callar.

Gaspar:

Yo me llamo Gaspar,
este otro Melchor, y éste Baltasar.
Rey, un rey ha nacido que es Señor de la Tierra
que mandará en el siglo en gran paz y sin guerra.

Herodes:

¿Es así de verdad?

Gaspar:

Sí, rey, por caridad.

Herodes:

¿Cómo lo habéis sabido?
¿Qué seña habéis tenido?

Gaspar:

> Rey, de verdad te diremos
> que ya bien lo sabemos.

Melchor:

> Una estrella es nacida
> que es gran maravilla.

Baltasar:

> La seña ha aparecido
> de que el rey ha nacido.

Herodes:

> ¿Cuánto ha que la visteis
> y así la percibisteis?

Gaspar:

> Hará unos trece días.

Herodes:

> Pues id y buscar,
> y al rey adorad,
> y luego tornad por aquí;
> que yo allá iré
> y le adoraré
> cuando sepa el camino a seguir.

(The Wise Men bow and exit, and now the notes of a piano are heard.)

Herod:

> ¿Otro rey sobre mí?
> Nunca tal cosa vi.
> Aún no soy muerto
> Ni bajo tierra puesto.
> El siglo va a la zaga
> y no sé qué me haga.
> En verdad no lo crea
> hasta que no lo vea.
> Vengan mis abades
> y mis potestades,
> y mis gramáticos,
> y mis estrelleros,
> y mis retóricos.
> Me dirán la verdad, si está en lo escrito,
> o si lo saben ellos, o si lo han sabido.

The king's court approaches him.

Escena V

(Herodes is surrounded by his court.)

Rabí:

> Rey, ¿qué es lo que deseas? Henos aquí
> reunidos.

Herodes:

> Oídme atentos todos, ¿traéis vuestros escritos?

Another learned man:

> Rey, sí que los traemos
> y los mejores que tenemos.

Herodes:

> Pues escuchad:
> Decidme la verdad,
> si aquel hombre ha nacido
> que estos tres reyes me han advertido.
> Di, Rabí, la verdad si tú lo has sabido.

Rabí:

> De veras os lo digo
> que no lo hallo escrito.

Another rabbi:

> Hamihala, que vienes engañado,
> ¿Por qué eres rabí de este modo llamado?
> No entiendes las profecías,
> las que nos dijo Jeremías.
> Por mi ley que estamos errados.
> ¿Por qué no estamos acordados?
> ¿Por qué no decimos la verdad?

Rabí:

> Yo no la sé, por caridad.

The other rabbi:

> Porque no la hemos deseado
> ni en nuestros libros buscado.
> Y por mi fe es verdadero

lo que estos reyes te dijeron.
Yo también allá iré,
y rogaré y le adoraré.
(The court exits.)

Escena VI

(On the right side of the stage, a group formed by shepherds, the Virgin,
Saint Joseph, and the manger appears still motionless, like an altarpiece.)

(An angel appears and sings alone)
(Music: N 9 Der Engel)
¡Gloria, Gloria, in excelsis!
Alegría pastores venid
y buena nueva a todos repartid.
Despierten pastores,
Por Cristo despertad
al Portal de Belén
corramos todos ya:
¡Corred, corred!
Del cielo desciendo y os traigo
Un mensaje de buena voluntad.
Alegría, pues, en este día,
Cantad la Nueva a la humanidad.. A la humanidad.. A la
humanidad…
Oh pastores, oh pastores no desesperéis,
la buena nueva yo os traeré
The angel speaks to the shepherds, who begin to wake up as the angel
sings.

Angel:
Venid, pastores, afuera,
a mirar al Dios nacido;
y al sonido del rabel
cantadle lindas endechas,
pues es hecha
la maravilla de siglos
esperada.
Venid, pastores, afuera,
por vuestro bien.

A shepherd:
Pues cierto nos guía

el ángel, iremos;
al Niño lleguemos
que ha poco nacía.
Con Ave María
la Madre alabemos
que a Su Majestad
en el vientre había;
pues cierto nos guía
el ángel, lleguemos.

Another shepherd:

Al son de panderos
y de castañuelas
bailad los cabreros.
Bailemos, por Dios,
frente al nuevo Sol,
el sol que reluce
aún más que el del cielo,
pues es el Sol de almas
y de entendimientos.

All the shepherds:

Al son de panderos
y de castañuelas,
bailad, los cabreros.

A selected group of six or more shepherds will dance a "jota."
At the end, the shepherds will exit the manger while bowing.
A different piano music begins, and the Wise Kings appear, walking
toward the manger.

Escena VII

Baltasar:

De cierto éste es el lugar
donde al Rey debemos hallar.

Gaspar:

Mirad allé recién bajado
el que es Señor de lo creado.

Melchor:

Bendito vientre de mujer
en donde Dios tomó el ser.

The Three Kings:
>Bendita seas, bendita eres
>entre todas las mujeres.
>They approach and worship the Child, leaving their gifts.

Gaspar:
>Yo del oro os traigo, o Rey de lo creado,
>la tierra os regala lo que vos le habéis dado.

Melchor:
>Yo, como hombre eres, la mirra te ofrecía,
>hijo del Hombre en brazos de la Virgen María.

Baltasar:
>Y yo, Señor de los cielos –Dios del poder inmenso-,
>os doy el homenaje del mundo del incienso.

The angel approaches and says:
>Adorad, oh reyes,
>adorad, pastores;
>los grandes y chicos,
>ángeles y hombres
>mi voz escuchad:
>Gloria a Dios en las alturas
>y paz en la tierra a las criaturas
>de buena voluntad.

The actors all follow the angel with the star and exit while singing a carol about the Wise Kings.

Seventh Grade

An example for seventh grade is "Los caballos de los conquistadores" by José Santos Chocano. The presentation example that we explained for sixth grade can be followed. Once the student has a picture of the strong, agile horses, with their slender necks, shiny croups, and musical hoofs, the poem takes on vigor and form.

To create a mental picture of the poem, it is important to give the student a frame of reference regarding the author, the landscape, and its spirit. In this case we have a song to beautiful and powerful animals. We can also speak of the Incas and the Andes. The recitation can be carried out in various ways, either by the whole class, by rows, by sex, or by dividing the class into groups, or even individually.

"Los caballos de los conquistadores"
by
José Santos Chocano

¡Los caballos eran fuertes!
¡Los caballos eran ágiles!
Sus pescuezos eran finos y sus ancas
relucientes y sus cascos musicales…
¡Los caballos eran fuertes!
¡Los caballos eran ágiles!
¡No! No han sido los guerreros solamente,
de corazas y penachos y tizonas y estandartes,
los que hicieron la conquista
de las selvas y los Andes;
los caballos andaluces, cuyos nervios
tienen chispa de la raza voladora de los árabes,
estamparon sus gloriosas herraduras
en los secos pedregales,
en los ríos resonantes,
en los húmedos pantanos,
en las nieves silenciosas,
en las pampas, en las sierras, en los bosques y en los valles.
¡Los caballos eran fuertes!
¡Los caballos eran ágiles!

A play can also be a good language class project. In this case, organization is very important. Once the play is selected, all the students should have a copy. The vocabulary should be presented, and the play should be discussed, including its meaning as well as the author's intention.

Eighth Grade

At this stage it is easier to introduce assonant rhyme (vowel rhyme), which is more typical of contemporary authors, because the students will be working more with the content and ways of expressing feelings. One can also use simple plays, or create and put on shadow plays.

One of the advantages of shadow theater is that it facilitates the participation of all the students. It is easy to manage, it helps the spectator to understand what is happening, and it encourages the participation of the less advanced students. For this project we select one or more stories that have several parts. The material is passed out, read, and discussed. Some musical pieces are chosen for the story or stories. This can be done in conjunction with the music teacher, and the pieces can be played in a group or individually. The parts are assigned: the narrator or narrators, the person in charge of special effects (such as music, sound of steps, rain effect), the puppeteers, those who will prepare the characters, those who will design the stage, those in charge of change of scenery.

Once everbody knows what they have to do, the work begins. The first job is the creation of the theater. It has to be light and portable (see drawing). It will have a stage covered with onionskin paper or thin tissue paper. A 100-watt bulb will be placed behind the stage to light up the screen.

The characters are prepared with black cardboard. The silhouette of the character is drawn with a white pencil. After it is cut out, the cardboard silhouette is attached with transparent tape to barbecue skewers, to hold and manipulate the puppet.

Each student will have to work independently on the role or task assigned. The students who narrate the story should have practiced beforehand, and the puppeteers should also have their lines almost memorized, so that both groups can now begin to practice together. The movement of the puppets, whether fast or slow, should be carefully practiced to bring about the desired stage effects.

Among the puppeteers, one of them may act as a prompter. Another person can be in charge of the change of puppeteers, or can be ready to substitute for them. The narrator and the musicians can be seated in view of the public. During the change of scenes, there can be music, either live or background recorded music, to maintain the interest of the spectators during the change of scenes.

Any story can be used, for example: "Sleeping Beauty," "Snow White and the Seven Dwarves," "The Three Little Goats," "The Little Lead Soldier," "The Three Bears," "The Piper of Hamelin," "Little Red Riding Hood," and many others in this vein. These stories capture the audience by facilitating understanding of what is happening, since most of them are well known.

These activities serve to encourage connections with the local Hispanic community, and can be presented as a community project. They can also be shown to students in the school's kindergarten, first and second grades, as a special presentation, or in one of the school festivals for public attendance.

122

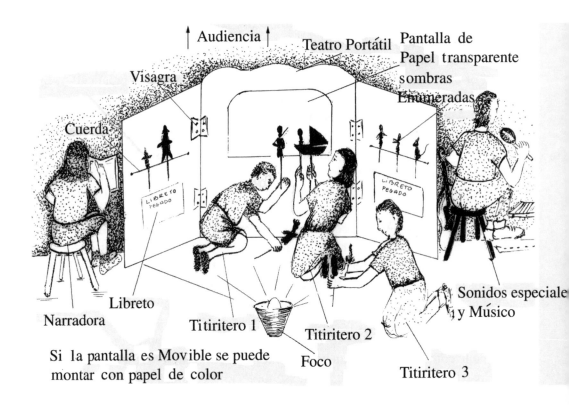

Example for *The Three Billy Goats:*

Las

Tres

Cabritas
Traviesas

124

Example for *The Tin Soldier:*

El Soldatito De Plomo

Chapter 5

Dances and Festivals

Dances

To maintain a balance in a language lesson, it is essential to apply the rhythm of contraction and expansion. One suitable method for achieving this objective is through dance. In dancing, the child not only learns to coordinate his movements rhythmically, but also enters the soul of another culture, through gesture and its expression of feeling.

Especially in the early grades, when the child's limb system is most alive, dance can serve not only as a vehicle of expression, but also one that integrates both motor and social coordination. In our present-day society, children grow up without feeling the expressiveness of folk dance, which was so strongly rooted in the past. The modern rhythm of life and the pressure it exerts on the individual have gradually displaced this means of harmonizing our faculties. Instead, sports have been emphasized as a way of channeling this energy, with no account taken of the missions that dance historically fulfilled in the growth of the child.

Historically, in the Latin American countries, the indigenous peoples would dance as a way of expressing their transcendental feelings about life and death. Little by little, with the arrival and domination of the Spaniards, dance, together with other native cultural expressions, became still more deeply rooted in daily life, as a way to re-establish ancestral ties. Dance became the vehicle for expressing vital feelings, customs, and the connection with the past.

With this impulse, the Latin American—coming from a people whose origin stems from a mixing of natives and colonizers—carries dance in his soul. It becomes a vital necessity, with a mystical meaning. Because of this, dance, however simple, is an expression of these sentiments.

In this sense, dance and its performance will occupy an important place in the language class, especially in the first five grades, when the child is disposed toward imitation and is less self-conscious. In the first two grades it is important to present dance in a circle, since the child still feels united with her surroundings. Gradually the circle takes on other forms, giving way to greater spatial freedom; at the same time the child, by means of movements and rhythms, will develop his motor skills. From fourth grade on, rhythmical changes are carried out requiring greater ability and attention to realize other kinds of movements, such as crossing the foot and hands, and body turns. This will help to achieve in the upper grades a greater autonomy with regard to expression, movement, and rhythm, not only in the physical realm, but also in the emotional and spiritual.

Recommendations for the Teaching of Dances

It must be stressed that the most important aspect of this activity is how the teacher conducts it and whether she can inspire pleasure and delight in dancing.

1   First, choose a grade that reacts to dance in a positive way (from first to fifth grade is ideal).

2   Work in conjunction with the main lesson teacher. It is important to enlist the assistance of the class teacher to help teach the cultural dance in the Spanish lesson, and to present it later at a festival or assembly. If the response is positive, we proceed to the instruction.

3   The dance is initially presented in small doses. During the Spanish class, we begin with basic movements, either at the beginning of the lesson, after the opening verse, or in the middle of the lesson, as a relaxing activity. If there is singing with the dance, this should be taught beforehand, so that the students will accompany themselves with the melody of the song. It must be kept in mind that the class is not purely a dance class; dance is just one of several activities that a pleasant class should have. Therefore, we should not overextend ourselves with the dance practice, otherwise we lose the attention of the students.

4   Once the dance has been presented in its totality, the class is divided into two groups and proceeds to a more intense practice. If the group is very big (20 or more students), or the space is limited, one group can practice with the teacher while the other works on a drawing related to the dance, or writes a poem in their Spanish notebooks, or carries out some other pertinent activity.

5   Finally, if the dance is still not polished, the Spanish teacher can ask the class teacher if extra practices can be done during other classes or during the main lesson. There are instances where the main lesson teacher likes to have these practices during the class period. If this is the case, the practice will not be quite so demanding for the Spanish teacher. Two teachers are then in control of the class, and this is ideal for the learning of this activity. The performance day arrives, and both teachers, Spanish and main lesson, should be responsible for everything going well. The Spanish teacher should give the audience a brief explanation of the historical aspect of the dance.

6   Costumes are very important so that the dance will stand out in all its splendor. They are important not only for the dance itself, but also because they help the students identify with the culture they are going to represent. Parents can be asked to contribute to the costumes with anything appropriate they may have at home; or a community project could be promoted, to begin making the costumes as part of the school wardrobe. With this kind of community project in mind, it would be necessary to begin organizing at least four months in advance.

7   The last recommendation, and perhaps the most important, is to always give a brief explanation, in the form of a story or history, about the dance's form, costumes, and origin. Since the student is curious about why he is being taught a certain activity, this explanation helps make the experience more meaningful and profound for him.

In the following pages we offer some examples of dances, taking into account the different cultures that make up the Spanish-speaking countries.

A video has been created for those who would like to visualize in greater detail the different dances and songs. The play *Los reyes aztecas* is also on this video. (Contact Carmita Luce.)

An Indigenous Dance

An example under this category is the "piama" dance, which comes from the Amazon region of Bolivia. It is to be noted that, in general, most of the indigenous dances from these regions have similarities. This dance is performed with the rhythm of "taquirari," a soft and melodious rhythm, a relaxing activity after the arduous work under the burning sun of that region. The woman carries a jug either on her head or on her left shoulder.

Vocabulary

The word "piama," meaning "give me," comes from a language called "arawak," an indigenous word, or "mojeña," which derives from the place of origin of this dance, San Ignacio de Moxos or Mojos. The word "tutuma," mentioned in the song, is another indigenous word designating a round and inedible fruit. After this fruit is cut from the tree, it is split in half, and all its fiber is extracted and allowed to dry in the sun. After several days the two halves of the "tutuma" have dried. The Indians use it as a vessel for pouring water from the rivers into the jugs, or to bathe themselves. In addition, landscapes are drawn on this artifact so that it can be used as decoration.

The word "taquirari" comes from the word "takirikire," which means "arrow," to be used to defend oneself from wild animals and also for daily sustenance from fishing and hunting. These Indians had a love for nature, and many artifacts were considered sacred motifs. This dance can be used already in third and fourth grades.

Song

PIAMA (indigenous song)	DAME (Spanish translation)
Piama, piama etanerida	Dame, dame mi "tutuma"
nicuti chayare chucurate.	para medir el chocolate.
No tei paresa samirai	Como soy pobre
nagi, nagiragi temunacanu	nadie me quiere.

Indigenous dance: the Piama and its choreography

This dance is very simple to learn, and consists of taking a step forward with the right foot and then another with the left foot, and so on successively. The shoulders move rhythmically also from right to left, always in time with the rhythm, which is accelerated in certain moments of the choreography.

The students enter the stage dancing in two rows, boys and girls. The boys put both hands behind them, and the girls hold the bottom part of their dresses lightly with the fingers of the right hand, and with the other hand they carry a jug on their left shoulder. When the song is about to be sung a second time, the girls go to one side and the boys to the other until they form a circle. Then the girls, still dancing, go to the center, leave their jugs, and return to their respective places. Up to this point the rhythm has been slow.

Now the song is sung a third time very rapidly, and the dance takes the form of a serpent all over the stage, alternating boy and girl. Since this movement is somewhat longer than the previous ones, singing and recitation of the words of the song are energetically combined in both languages (Spanish and arahuac). At all times one should try to convey the feeling of the Indian to the soul of the child, so that the experience of this event may acquire a greater enrichment.

At the end, all the boys slowly form a row while dancing, and the girls pick up their jugs and form another row. In this way they get ready to leave the stage dancing.

The clothes for this dance are represented in the following drawings, for both girls and boys. After that, there is a drawing of a "tutuma", a jug to be used with water or chocolate, decorated with a tropical landscape.

Drawings by sixth-grade students from
the Waldorf School of the Peninsula.

This dance could be learned in the fourth grade. If possible, one should learn to play the castanets, not perfectly, but well enough to accompany a song. This musical instrument, which is very Spanish, will penetrate the feelings of the child. Beforehand, two traditional and popular Christmas carols are taught, *Los peces en el río* and *Dime niño*. With the song *Dime niño*, we are teaching a dance of Celtiberian origin based on the *jota*. Historically this dance, performed generally by the common people, is an expression of Spanish folklore; the dance overcomes the emotions, enlivens the senses, and stimulates harmony of forms and movements, skill and vigor, and also at the same time, fineness and subtlety.

Given the origin of this dance, children are able to capture in a certain way the harmony and delicacy of the movements of the *jota*.

The performance is elaborated in the following way: the whole class appears onstage, dispersed, making a lot of noise, talking to each other in loud voices and wishing each other a merry Christmas. After a few minutes, the class forms a semi-circle, with the girls in the center and the boys on both sides. Immediately they take their castanets from little baskets and begin to play them while singing *Los peces en el río*. The accompaniment with this instrument usually occurs only when they sing the part of the chorus. For the second part, the boys separate a little from the girls to proceed with the song and dance *Dime niño*. The boys begin to sing at the same time as the girls, and they dance the choreography of the dance, similar to the *jota*. When they get to the part of the chorus, the children continue singing, but this time they accompany the song with the castanets.

Choreography for the Spanish Jota: Dime niño

Before beginning the choreography, we explain briefly and simply the basic main step of this graceful dance. We hold both arms up, and when the song begins, the girls on tiptoe raise their right foot toward the left foot, while at the same time they lower the left arm, touching the other one. They continue moving, doing the opposite, and viceversa. This movement is like a gentle, delicate jump, appropriate for expressing the festivity of the arrival of the little redeemer.

With the step mentioned above, the girls begin this Celtiberian dance until they form a circle. Then in the part of the chorus "resuenan con alegría…" and without moving, they proceed with the same step, with the difference that they they knock the floor three times with their feet at the end of the song's chorus.

Next comes an interweaving part that has a different but fairly simple step. This interweaving requires an even number of dancers. As a point of departure, two girls are assigned as guides for two groups that face each other and the rest behind the assigned group. In this way they weave in and out, greeting each other with their palms and moving their heads slightly from side to side as they enter and leave the circle.

With this movement, the girls separate out, following in a row a guide who will lead them toward the audience. With the girls in the center, and the boys kneeling on either side, with their arms up high, they recite the poem "Paz", as an expression of love and peace.

"Paz"

Si en el corazón de los hombres
está el sentimiento de la guerra,
educad ese corazón
en el sentimiento de la paz.

Si en el espíritu de los hombres
está el espíritu de la guerra;
cambiadlo por el espíritu de la paz.

Si la ambición negativa y desmedida
de los hombres llevan a la guerra,
trocad esa ambición en positiva
que lleven a la paz.

Si la esclavitud idealista
origina la guerra,
educad la libertad de convicciones.

El espíritu bélico es de mediocres,
equivocados, elevad y corregid esos
espíritus y fructificará la paz.

"Dime niño"
(traditional Christmas song)

Dime niño
¿de quién eres,
todo vestidito de blanco?
Soy de la Virgen María
(se repite)
y del Espíritu Santo.
Resuenan con alegría
los cánticos de mi tierra   (Coro)
y vive el Niño Jesús
que ha nacido en Nochebuena.
La Nochebuena viene
tu ru ru
la Nochebuena se va
y nosotros cantaremos
de la felicidad.
Resuenan…(Coro)

Los peces en el río
(traditional Christmas song)

Coro:

   Am   Dm
Pero mira como brbrn los peces en el río
                  E7   Am
pero mira como beben al ver Dios nacido.
           Dm
Beben y beben y vuelven a beber
              E7   Am
los peces en el río al ver al Dios nacer.

         E7
La Virgen se está peinando
         Am
entre cortina y cortina
         E7
Las cortinas son de oro
         Am
y el peine de plata fina.

Coro:

            E7
La Virgen está lavando
            Am
con un poquito de jabón.
            E7
Se le quemaron las manos
          A   M
manos de mi corazón.

Coro:

            E7
La Virgen está lavando
            AM
y tendiendo en el romero.
            E7
Los angelitos cantando
            Am
y el romero floreciendo.

Next, there are examples of the clothes for "La Jota," for both boys and girls.

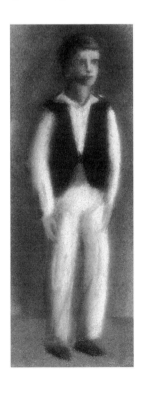  

The drawing and pastel are by sixth-grade students from the Waldorf School of the Peninsula.

Drawings by sixth-grade students from the Waldorf School of the Peninsula.

Dance for the Mexican Song: De colores

This is an example of the ethnic mosaic in dancing. The song *De colores*, can be taught in first grade, and is received with enthusiasm, because of its words, as well as its soft, gentle melody, which is easy to express in the form of a dance, with characteristics of a possible waltz. At this stage of childhood there emanates a kind of natural shyness, and this is why it is essential to have movement in a circle, to give greater security to the child in the performance of the choreography.

Choreography

The students are placed in a circle, alternating by sex. The girl takes her skirt in her hands and the boy places his behind his back. Then they begin to sing the song while turning in a circle. At a certain part of the song, depending on the choreography, they turn around and move in the other direction. Then, when they sing the part of the chorus "y por eso los grandes amores…" they hold hands and move toward the center and back again, following the beat of the melody with their arms going up and down. Here one has the impression of the opening and closing of a flower in spring.

The second part of the choreography begins with "canta el gallo," and at this point the boys, still in a circle, look at their assigned partners; then they all turn around at the same time to look again at their partners.

To coordinate this, one should use certain words in the song as a signal to turn around. Once they have done this, they wait for a moment in their places, still dancing, and then proceed to cross again in order to return to their original places.

Finally, when the chorus part is sung again, they do the same as before with the only difference that, in the repetition of the chorus, the children let go of each other's hands, and turn toward the audience. Then, as a kind of greeting and goodbye, they continue dancing forward and backward, with their arms still going up and down.

In this way the dance ends, having provided an entertaining and joyful experience for the children.

"De colores"

De colores
de colores se visten los campos en la primavera
de colores
de colores son los pajaritos que vienen de fuera
de colores
de colores es el arcoiris que vemos lucir
y por eso los grandes amores de muchos amores
me gustan a mí
y por eso los grandes amores de muchos colores
me gustan a mí
canta el gallo
canta el gallo con el quiri, quiri, quiri, quiri, quiri
la gallina
la gallina con el kara, kara, kara, kara, kara
los polluelos
los polluelos con el pío, pío, pío, pío, pío
y por eso los grandes amores de muchos colores
me gustan a mí
y por eso los grandes amores de muchos colores
me gustan a mí

Next there is an example of the clothes used for "De Colores". The boy's dress is very similar to that used for the dance "Piama".

Festivals

Festivals give us the opportunity to connect with spiritual forces that are a part of our daily life. They also help us to relate to other people within our community. When we plan a festival we should be open to changes and be flexible with our goals. It is very important to transmit through poems, songs, and dances, the spirit of the festival. The rhythm of the year should be interrupted by the festivals, which in the school are related to both the curriculum and the seasons. During the spring and summer we breathe out in the most extroverted way. The fall and winter is the time when we breathe in, when the days are darker and colder and we are more introspective. It is the time when we work on our inner life, when we have quieter moments. Keeping in mind the changing seasons, Waldorf schools celebrate different festivals. Some are organized for the community (Halloween, May Day, and plays during Christmas season); others are organized just for students during an assembly (Saint Nicholas, Michaelmas). As Spanish teachers, we should look for appropriate festivals to celebrate during the year. These will depend on the place or country where the school is located, and the origin of the teacher. In winter, the birth of Jesus is celebrated in the Christian calendar and in Waldorf schools of the northern hemisphere. With the beginning of Advent, the students walk in a spiral, carrying candles, bringing the light with great spiritual absorption. Also during this season many schools put on Christmas performances.

Below we offer examples carried out by some California teachers in their Spanish classes.

Las Posadas

"Las Posadas" (the Inns) is an example of one of many such festivals that can be celebrated at this time of the year. It is of Mexican origin, and for teachers who live in areas where the Mexican population is high, it is an appropriate celebration.

The "Posadas" begin the 16th of December, and the processions take place for nine days. They represent Mary and Joseph looking for a place to spend the night and give birth to the infant Jesus. In many towns the "Posadas" are performed by children who carry candles and a platform with the figures of Joseph and Mary, to which is added the figure of baby Jesus on December 24th. A girl is dressed as Mary and a boy as Joseph, and they go at the front of the procession, which goes from house to house asking if there is any room for lodging. They sing a song imploring to be given a place to spend the night. The children inside the house respond with a song telling them to look elsewhere, because they have no room. After going to several houses, they are accepted and invited to come in. Several prayers are said, and everybody approaches the table to eat. After the meal, all the children have a piñata party.

As Spanish teachers, we can take advantage of this nice festival and perform it at school. We can choose two grades—third and fourth. One represents Mary and Joseph looking for a place to spend the night, and the other is the group that invites them to come in. The third grade goes from classroom to classroom singing the song of the posadas; they will also sing that there is no room for Mary and Joseph. Only the fourth grade invites them to come in. The house will be decorated to receive them, and the pupils will prepare something to eat and drink. Each class will sing some Christmas carols they have learned and then they all eat together. After eating they break the piñata that the class made for this occasion.

Here is a poem that the students can learn to recite or read:

Nueve días antes de Navidad,
todos con felicidad
celebramos Las Posadas
con nuestra gente amada.
Vamos de casa en casa
pidiendo un lugar,
así María y José pueden esperar,
al niño que va a llegar.
En ninguna casa nos aceptarán,
todos contestarán:
¡Aquí no hay lugar!
Sólo en una nos dirán:
¡Por favor, quédense acá!
Allí nos quedaremos
y todos cantaremos:
"No quiero oro,
no quiero plata,
yo sólo quiero romper la piñata."

January 6th is the Day of the Three Wise Men, that is, the day when the three Kings on camels arrive at Bethlehem to worship the Child Jesus and give him a present. In Hispanic countries, the children also receive a present from the Kings. They leave their shoes at the door of the house, together with water and food for the camels. The next day there is a gift in each shoe. On that day a special, ring-shaped bread called the "Rosca de Reyes" is prepared. It has inside a tiny doll, which is supposed to bring good luck to whoever gets the slice that contains it. An activity of this day could be for the teacher to bring in a "rosca" to share with the class, or perform the *Three King's Play* in the 6th grade class in Spanish as suggested in Chapter 4.

El Día de los Muertos (The Day of the Dead, or All Souls Day)

The feast of All Souls Day is a tribute to the beauty, the venera-tion, and also the humor of the concept of death. Its celebration is hom-age to those who have died. It begins on October 31, the day when the souls of deceased children return to their homes. To receive them, the family prepares an altar with belongings and mementos of the child when he was alive: the favorite toy, food, candies, flowers, candles, photo-graphs, etc.

The first of November is when the souls of deceased adults re-turn to their homes. The altar is decorated with photos, fancy dishes of food, fruit, breads, and small objects that recall the honored person. On November 2nd, all the families go to the cemetery, carrying flowers and the prepared food. They walk in a procession through the streets, leaving a trail of petals so the spirits can find a path to follow. Upon arriving at the cemetery, they place salt and water in small jars on the tombs, as well as the food that they have brought. There they sing, pray, dance, and eat all night long, together with friends and relatives, remembering their loved ones. Then they pick up everything and return to their homes.

In Waldorf schools, the festival of Halloween is usually celebrated. Some classes prepare different activities with the children. As All Souls Day begins on Halloween day; it is a very good occasion to prepare the altar, so the community will have an opportunity to absorb a little of Mexican culture. Each class can prepare and bring something different to put on the altar, for example, paper flowers, fruits and vegetables, clay skeletons, photos of loved ones, candles, incense, fresh flowers, etc. Af-ter the altar is prepared, the teacher or a Spanish-speaking parent can explain how other people celebrate this day. Another alternative is for each class to have its own altar.

When it is carried out by grades, it is recommended that the fes-tival should be done from sixth grade on. This activity is a good opportu-nity for the student to speak about the person he or she is honoring. If he doesn't want to present a member of the family, he can choose a histori-cal character, an artist, an athlete, a political leader, or someone admired, and carry out a small research on the life of that person. As class activi-ties, paper flowers, etc., can be prepared a week before, and the decora-tion for the altar can be planned. The student will have a unique experi-ence and at the same time will learn about this Mexican tradition.

We should keep in mind that if we want to have the community participate, the preparations will be greater, and we will need to consult with the main lesson teachers, especially in the lower grades. It will like-wise be necessary to begin organizing the community participation with enough time, coordinating how and in what way each class will partici-pate.

Chapter 6

Other Resources

A Selected, Annotated Bibliography on
Foreign Languages in Waldorf Schools

Prepared by Michael Navascués

The following bibliography has been prepared in the hope that it will be of practical, pedagogical value to Waldorf foreign language teachers, especially those in the early stages of their work, or those who may be preparing themselves for this area of teaching. Seasoned teachers may also wish to consult it. In addition, foreign language teachers in mainstream schools, some of which are currently reconsidering the benefits of early language training, can find here useful information and sources on an educational movement that has long had a unique commitment to the early learning of languages.

Published material on the Waldorf approach to foreign language instruction is scattered among many different sources, most of which are rather brief. This list covers only references published in English, as many as I was able to locate. Included are the important indications on foreign language by the founder of the Waldorf movement, Rudolf Steiner, as well as those by some more recent Waldorf educators. Several of the works cited contain few or even no references to foreign language, but have been included as useful introductions to Waldorf theory and practice. Foreign language teachers without Waldorf training will find that study of such works will be indispensable for integrating their work effectively into a Waldorf school setting.

Comments following each entry refer briefly to the content and to specific passages on foreign language. Opinions about the entries are strictly my own. Page numbers in parentheses refer to sections on foreign language or language in general. Chapter numbers or titles are included to orient readers whose editions of the book may be different. Specific resources for Spanish teachers are contained in the bibliography at the end of this book.

Aeppli, Willi. *Rudolf Steiner Education and the Developing Child.* Trans. Angelika V. Ritscher-Hill. Hudson, NY: Anthrosophic Press, 1986. 207pp. First published in 1934, it deals with a wealth of class experiences and reflections of a Waldorf teacher in Switzerland. The chapter "Teaching Grammar" (138-154) is a fascinating account of how grammar was approached in a vivid, meaningful way. The author's methods can be inspiring and pertinent to foreign language teachers as well. Elaborates on Steiner's views on connection of verbs, adjectives, and nouns with willing, feeling, and thinking. Wonderful discussion of verb tenses. Recommended for imaginative insights.

Alexander, Sibylle. "The most Precious Gift of All." *Child and Man: Journal for Waldorf Education* vol. 16 no.1 (1982): 9-12. Deals largely with problem of "frustrated" beginners, children whose foreign language skills have not kept up with those of other classmates, or who have had difficulties because of a change of teachers. She offers methods for evaluating pupils and determining weaknesses. Methods can be used also as learning devices.

Edmunds, Francis L. *Rudolf Steiner Education.* London: Rudolf Steiner Press, 1962. 101 pp. Eloquent introduction to Waldorf education and philosophy by a well-known British educator. Relatively few particulars on the curriculum, nothing on foreign language.

Everett, Roland. "Language Teaching in a Waldorf School." *Child and Man: Journal for Waldorf Education* vol. 16 No. 1 (1982): 5-8 Brief remarks on the ease and joy with which "children under nine absorb a language entirely through the ear, out of their feeling for sounds and also through activity games, but never through conscious comprehension" (p.6). Some considerations on grammar and the problem of finding appropriate German literature for adolescents.

Harwood, A.C. *The Recovery of Man in Childhood: a Study in the Educational Work of Rudolf Steiner.* London: Hodder and

Stoughton, 1969. 211 pp. By an eminent British Waldorf educator, this is a wide-ranging discussion of Steiner's child psychology and its pedagogical applications. Chapter XII (pp. 135-140) deals with foreign languages; about half the chapter is devoted to the teaching of Latin and Greek, taken up in some Waldorf schools in the fifth and sixth grades. He notes "the happy fact that children remain a little younger in foreign languages, and will be content to continue with fairytale plays and fables later than in their own tongue... A lost childhood can in part be recovered in the nursery rhymes and songs and tales of a foreign tongue." (p.136)

Lipton, Gladys C. *Practical Handbook to Elementary Foreign Language Programs*, 2nd ed. Lincolnwood, IL: National Textbook Company, 1992. The author is an authority on FLES, or Foreign Language in the Elementary School, which in recent years has experienced a revival in some parts of the U.S. Much of the book provides advice on how to promote and develop FLES in public schools. Chapters 8, 9, and 10 give sketchy summaries of methodologies. Waldorf teachers will note a number of suggestions and teaching strategies long practiced in Waldorf language classes: no formal grammar in early stages, learning through motion ("Total Physical Response"), use of song, poetry, folktales, and biographies, non-dependence on textbooks, etc. Extensive bibliographies.

Navascués, Michael. "Foreign Languages in American Waldorf Schools." *Renewal: A Journal for Waldorf Education.* Fall/Winter (1993): 27-30. Brief overview of Waldorf approach to foreign language education.

—. "Waldorf Schools: Seventy-Six Years of Early Language Learning." *Learning Languages: The Journal of the National Network for Early Language Learning.* Vol. 2, No. 2 (Winter 1997): 34-42. Introduction to Waldorf foreign language pedagogy and the place of languages in American Waldorf schools. Article is written for the mainstream language teaching profession.

Querido, René M. *Creativity in Education: the Waldorf Approach.*San Francisco: H.S. Dakin Company, 1984. 87 pp. Brief volume based on a lecture series by a noted Waldorf educator who once taught languages. Highly readable, with humor and warmth, it contains a lively chapter on foreign language teaching (Ch. 7, 71-83) of great interest. Chapter 2 has a discussion of the four temperaments in children. Recommended for all language teachers.

Spock, Marjorie. *Teaching as a Lively Art.* Hudson, NY: Anthroposophic Press, 1985. 137 pp. Concise explanation of the Waldorf curriculum and the child's stages of growth from grades 1 to 8. Written with clarity and enthusiasm, it contains occasional brief references to foreign language. Bibliography of Waldorf education. Recommended as a readable overview of the curriculum year by year.

Steiner, Rudolf. *The Child's Changing Consciousness and Waldorf Education.* 8 Lectures, Dornach, 1923. Trans. Roland Everett. Hudson, NY: Anthroposophic Press; London: Rudolf Steiner Press, 1988. 239 pp. Although it has no pertinent information on foreign language, it is an excellent overview of Steiner's ideas on Waldorf education and education in general, while he was developing them in the first Waldorf school. Clear picture of concept of child development and relation to education. Smooth translation. The foreword by Douglas Sloan is commended to educators and readers unfamiliar with Steiner's pioneering insights.

—. *Discussions with Teachers.* 15 discussions, Stuttgart, 1919. Trans. Helen Fox. London: Rudolf Steiner Press, 1967. 166 pp. Steiner indicates that the choice of foreign language for children cannot be governed by theoretical considerations, but rather by what they need to make their way in the world (p.59). In another passage, he stresses the need for a "kindly, gentle" approach on the part of the foreign language teacher, to build trust and confidence (p.161). He recommends readings of a lyric-epic nature for ages 12 to 15. Criticism of the modern passion for giving children frequent marks and report cards, which are of small significance in a Waldorf school (pp. 162-163).

—. *The Education of the Child in the Light of Anthroposophy.* Trans. George and Mary Adams. 2nd ed. London: Rudolf Steiner Press, 1985. 48 pp. This early essay, first published in 1909 ten years before the opening of the first Waldorf school, is an outline of Steiner's ideas on the physical and spiritual nature of the developing child, and the far-reaching implications for education. No curricular specifics, but an essential introduction to the Waldorf concept of the three stages in child development.

—. *Human Values in Education.* 10 Lectures, Arnheim, Holland, 1924. Trans. Vera Compton-Burnett. London: Rudolf Steiner Press, 1971. Similar to Steiner's other lecture cycles on Waldorf education; lacks indications on foreign language teaching. Lecture 8 contains a glimpse of Steiner's view on the different qualities in languages, contrasting German and Italian (pp. 152-153).

—. *The Kingdom of Childhood.* 7 Lectures, Torquay, Great Britain, 1924. Trans. Helen Fox. Letchworth, Hertfordshire (U.K.): The Garden City Press Ltd., 1982. 159 pp. Given to a group of British teachers embarking on the first Waldorf school in England. Abundant advice to the class (main lesson) teacher, and references to Steiner's spiritual concepts, for which some study of basic anthroposophical works would be advisable. Lecture VI contains several pages on language and teaching foreign languages (pp. 117-123). He emphasizes the need to teach through the child's feelings, without translation or analysis, up to the ninth or tenth year, when self-awareness develops. Vowels express feelings, consonants relate to external world. Example of different nuance of meaning in words of different languages.

—. *Practical Advice to Teachers.* 14 Lectures, Stuttgart, 1919. Trans. Johanna Collis. 2nd ed. London: Rudolf Steiner Press, 1976. 205 pp. Lectures to the first teachers of the first Waldorf school. Several contain some of Steiner's views on language, and on the teaching of foreign languages. Lecture 2 (pp. 26-33) touches on his concept of vowels and consonants. Lecture 3 has interesting observations on poetry. Lecture 4 (pp. 63-69) is a unique interpretation of our relation to nouns, verbs, and adjectives. Lecture 9 (pp. 128-140) deals largely with problems of teaching foreign language; stresses avoidance of translation and rigid grammatical instruction, and the need to engage pupils in conversation. Lecture 10 (pp. 145-150) continues discussion of foreign language with advice on teaching auditory comprehension, homework, and practical writing tasks. These indications, although aphoristic and incomplete, seem to form the basis for subsequent development of Waldorf approaches to foreign language teaching and learning. Highly recommended for language teachers.

—. *Rudolf Steiner's Conferences with the Teachers of the Waldorf School in Stuttgart 1922-23*. Vol. 3. Trans. Pauline Wehrle. East Sussex (U.K.): Steiner Schools Fellowship, 1986. Conference of Feb. 6, 1923 makes reference to teaching foreign language and grammar (pp. 82-83). Reveals Steiner's disdain for the "untransformed terminology" of grammar, and the dull, pedantic way in which it was taught. Life must flow into the teaching of grammar.

—. *Soul Economy and Waldorf Education*. 16 Lectures, Dornach, 1921-22. Trans. Roland Everett. Spring Valley, NY: Anthroposophic Press; London: Rudolf Steiner Press, 1986. 349 pp. Familiarity with some of Steiner's basic books on spiritual cognition would facilitate understanding of these lectures. Lectures VII to XII deal with his complex views on physical and psychological-spiritual development from early childhood through adolescence. Many useful insights for Waldorf teachers. Lectures VIII and XII contain short but very important references to teaching foreign languages, as well as the mother tongue, and should be studied in their entirety (see especially pp. 126-127 and 211-215). Steiner is an early proponent of the "direct" or "natural" methods of teaching foreign language to children. Translation is to be avoided, and grammar study should not be introduced until around the tenth year.

Stockmeyer, Karl. *Rudolf Steiner's Curriculum for Waldorf Schools*. Trans. Roland Everett-Zade. Stourbridge (U.K.): Steiner Schools Fellowship Publications, 1991. 176 pp. Stockmeyer has compiled, organized, and commented on numerous quotations by Rudolf Steiner, drawn from his discussions with the first Waldorf faculty and from various other lectures on education. The constant interspersing of quotes by Steiner and commentaries by Stockmeyer creates a somewhat disjointed reading experience, but the book is a fascinating account of Steiner's multifacted involvement in developing the first school. Chapter 3, "Language Lessons" (pp. 43-54) is recommended for all Waldorf foreign language teachers. He insists on an oral, non-written approach for the first three grades. Facility for acquiring a language in a natural way declines from age 6 or 7 on. Many interesting insights and fragmentary comments on curriculum.

Stott, Michael. *Foreign Language Teaching in Rudolf Steiner Schools. Guidelines for class-teachers and language teachers.* Stroud, Gloucestershire (U.K.): Hawthorn Press, 1995. 142 pp. The first book in English on the topic. Practical discussion of foreign language lessons, with useful though brief comments on the teaching of grammar, vocabulary, and reading. Many samples and quotations in German and French, including a collection of play lets for the language classes. No detailed discussion of grade-by-grade curriculum, but a helpful, concise resource, especially for German and French teachers.

Bibliography and Reference Books

In its own way, a bibliography is always but an isolated photograph out of the writer's album. How many books, manuscripts, loose phrases, conversations between mind and paper, and ideas wrestled with over time are left out, impossible to cite in a catalogue of written sources? What of the books that, though not directly relevant to the topic at hand, have helped to shape the author's thinking? We will never know. What we can claim with assurance is that, while the list is a partial one, the sources cited below have passed through our hands and are legitimate. We trust in you, gentle reader, to view the following list in the spirit that you would view a few select photographs from an album, and to forgive any omissions.

The present bibliography is divided into the following sections:
1   Bibliography for *Senderos*: books used in the writing of *Senderos.*
2   Books used for *Imaginary Trips* (in Chapter 3, for 5th grade).
3   Reference books on the Spanish language.
4   Resource books for grades one to eight.
5   Series of Hispanic biographies.
6   Resource books for poetry, dramatization, and recitation.
7   Resource books for dances, folklore, and various activities.

1. Bibliography for Senderos

1. Belenson, Mel (Translator) *Working Material for the Class Teacher*. Study Material of the Pedagogical Section and the Pedagogical Research Center. Printed as a Manuscript 1994.

2. Bravo Villasante, Carmen. *Antología de la literatura infantil española* Editorial Doncel, Madrid. 1983.

3. Darío, Rubén, *Margarita*. Ediciones Ekaré. Banco del Libro, 8va. impresión, Venezuela, 1997.

4. EDEBE Lecturas. *Fábula del león y el ratón*. Editorial Edebe Barcelona, 1996.

4. Glas, Werner, *Speech Education in the Primary Grades of Waldorf Schools*. Sunbridge College Press, USA. 1982.

5. Kiersch, Johannes. *Language Teaching in Steiner Waldorf Schools*. Steiner Fellowship Publications. Kidrook Park, UK. 1997.

6. Kuhlerwind, George. *The Life of the Soul*. Traducido por George Kuhlerwind en 1982. Stuttgard, Alemania. Traducción revisada en 1990. Lindisfarne Press. Hudson, USA.

7. Ogletree, Earl. *Introduction to Waldorf Education. Curriculum and Methods*. University Press of America. Washington, D.C., 1979.

8. Paz, Octavio. *El Laberinto de la soledad y ostras abras*. Penguin Books, U.S.A. 1997.

9. Querido, René. *Creativity in Education*. H.S. Dakin Company, S.F. 1987.

10. Steiner, Rudolf. *Balance in Teaching*. Mercury Press. New York, 1990.
    - *A Modern Art of Education*. R. Steiner Press, London, U.K., 1981.
    - *Conferences with Teachers of the Waldorf School in Stuttgart*. R. Steiner, Fellowship Publications, Sussex, U.K., 1986.
    - *Faculty Meetings with Rudolf Steiner. Foundations of Waldorf Education*. Volume I: 1919 - 1922. Volume II: 1922 - 1924. Traducido por Robert Lathe andNancy Parsons Whitaker. Anthroposophic Press. Hudson. NY. 1998.
    - *Practical Course for Teachers*. R. Steiner Publishing Co. London, 1973.

- *Six Lectures on Language.* Stuttgart. December 1919, January 3 1920. Translated by Gertrude Teutsch. R. Steiner College, Fair Oaks, CA.
- *Study of Man.* R. Steiner Press, London, U.K., 1966.
- *The Kingdom of Childhood. Introductory Talks on Waldorf Education.* Traducción original de by Helen Fox. Anthroposophic Press. Hudson. NY., 1982.
- *The Genius of Language.* Anthroposophic Press. Hudson, N.Y. 1995.
- *Waldorf for Adolescence.* Steiner Schools Fellowship Publications. Sussex, U.K., 1993.

11. Stockemeyer, Karl E. A. *Rudolf Steiner's Curriculum for Waldorf Schools.* Steiner Fellowships Publications, Michael Hall Clunies. Ross Press, Bournemouth. U.K., 1985.

12. Von Sivers, Marie Steiner. *Creative Speech.The Nature of Speech Formation.* R. Steiner Press, London, U.K., 1978.

13. Walqui-van Lier, Barraza, Ruth. *Sendas Literarias.* Editorial Heinle and Heinle. Boston, 1995

14. Wilkinson, Roy. *The Origin and Development of Language.* Hawthorn Press, 1992.

2. Books used for "Imaginary Trips"

1. Fernandez, Eugenio. *Arte y Mitología de los indios Tainos de las Antillas Mayores.* Ediciones El Cemí, San Juan, Puerto Rico, 1979.

2. Gómez, Labor & Ballestero, Manuel. *Culturas indígenas de Puerto Rico.* Editorial Cultural, Inc., Río Piedras, Puerto Rico, 1978.

3. López, Morales; Rodriguez, Fonseca; Vazquez, Asencio y de Jesús, Arvelo. *Español, lengua viva.* Libro de Lectura # 3, 4, 5, 6. Editorial La Muralla, Madrid, 1995.

4. Colecciones Puertorriqueñas:
    Historia ilustrada de un pueblo, Fernández Mendez, Eugenio.
    Voz folklórica de Puerto Rico, Rosa Nieves, Cesareo.
    Lecturas Puertorriqueñas: prosa, Arce de Vázquz, Margot & Robles de Cardona, Mariana. Caribe Grolier, Inc., San Juan, Puerto Rico, 1991.

5. Sued - Badillo, Jalil. *La mujer indígena y su sociedad*. Editorial Antillana, Ría Piedras, Puerto Rico, 1979.

3. Reference Books on the Spanish Language

1. Seco, Manuel. *Gramática esencial del español*. Aguilar. Madrid, 1966.

2. Seco, Rafael. *Manual de gramática española*. Aguilar. Madrid, 1967.

3. Holt, Marion & Dueber, Julianne. *1001 Pitfalls in Spanish*. Barron's Educational Series, Inc., New York, 1997.

4. Kendris, Christopher. *501 Spanish Verbs, fully Conjugated in all Tenses*. Barrons's Educational Series, Inc., New York, 1990.

4. Resource Books Recommended for the Grades

First Grade

1. Kohen, Clarita. *Pajaritos*. Laredo Publishing Company Inc., Torrace, CA 1993.

2. Singer, Marlyn. *En el palacio del rey del océano*. Simon & Schuster, New York, 1995.

3. Transedition Books. *Cuentos de hadas*. Edición en Español. División de Andrómeda Oxford Limited. Courier Companies Inc., 1990.

4. Vazquez, Elbia. *El Coquí explorador, Libro 1: ¿Quiénes hacen la arena?* Taller Gráfico Góngoli, Puerto Rico, 1991.

Second Grade

5. Ada Alma Flor. *Como nació el arco iris*. Santillana. California, 1991.
   - *Medio pollito*. Bantam Doubleday Publiching Group, Inc., New York, 1995.

6. De Paola, Tomie. *Francis, the Poor Man of Assisi*. Holiday House, New York, New York, 1982.
   - *Nuestra Señora de Guadalupe*. Holiday House, New York, New York, 1980.

7. Elizagaray, Alga María. *Fábulas del Caribe*. Editorial Amaquemecan, Mexico, segunda imp., 1998.

8. Hamilton, Roland. *Fable for Beginning Spanish.* San José State University. Custum Publishers, 1996.

9. Vinyes, Jordi. *La leyenda de San Jorge.* Galera, Barcelona, 1986.

10. Zubizarreta, Rosalma; Rohmer, Harriet; Schecter, David. *The Woman who Outshone the Sun.* Children's Press.San Francisco, CA, 1987.

Third Grade
11. Ada, Alma Flor. *Gathering of the Sun.* Lothrop, Lee & Shepaud Books NY, 1997.

12. Alonso, Fernando. *Mateo y los Reyes Magos.* Santillana, S.A., Madrid, 1995.

13. Atman, Linda. *El Camino de Amelia.* Lees's Low Books Inc., New York, 1993.

14. Bornemann, Elsa I. *Poesía infantil.* Plus Ultra, Argentina, 1983.

15. Castañeda, Omar S. *El tapíz de la abuela.* Lee & Low Books Inc New York, 1993. Traducción al español de Aida E. Marcuse.

16. Cohen, Caron Lee. *El poni de barro.* Scholastic, New York, 1992. De Paola, Tomie. *La leyenda de la flor de nochebuena.* G.P. Putnam's Son, New York, 1994.

17. Dorros, Arthur. *Esta es mi casa.* Scholastic, USA, 1993.

18. Fearon Teacher Aids. *Un cuento de Quetzalcóatl acerca del chocolate.* USA. 1994.

19. Garza, Carmen. *Family Pictures.* Children's Books Press. S.F., CA, 1990.

20. Kurjian, Judi. *En mi propio jardín.* Charlesbridge Publishing, MA, USA, 1994.

21. Messenger, Norman. *Annabel's House.* Orchard Books. A. Division of Franklin Watts. NY, 1989.

22. Zendera, C. *Yací y su muñeca.* Editorial Juventud, Barcelona, 1974.

Fourth Grade

23. Grau, María. *Viva la lectura.* Grupo Editorial Norma Educativa. Catano. Puerto Rico.1995.

24. *EDEBE Lecturas. Fábula el león y el ratón.* Editorial Edebe Barcelona, 1996.

25. EGB Antos. *Lecturas y comentarios de 1, 2, 3, 4.* Editorial Anaya, Madrid, 1990.

26. El Libro de los Recortes. *Libro de lectura 10, 11, 12 años.* Ediciones Discadalia, Madrid, 1989.

27. Guzman, Rosa. *¡Viva la lectura!* Grupo Editorial Norma Educativa. Puerto Rico, 1995.

28. *Popol Vuh.* Simon & Schuster, New York, 1985.

29. Delacré, Lulú. *El gallo de bodas.* Scholastic, USA, 1994.

30. Linse, Barbara. *California's Hispanic Roots for Kids.* 80 Piedmont Court. Larkspur, CA, 1995.

31. Lowman, Hubert A. *The Old Spanish Missions of California.* LMG Crocker International, Honk Kong, 1996.

Fifth Grade

32. Cherry, Lynne. *El gran copoquero: un cuento de la selva amazónica.* Traducido por Alma Flor Ada. Libros viajeros, Harcourt Brace & Company: San Diego, N.Y., London, 1994.

33. De Lacré, Lulú. *Golden Tales: Myth, Legends, and Folktales from Latin America.* Scholastic Resources, New York, 1996.

34. Sword Bishop, Dorothy. *Ya sé leer.* NTC, Illinois, USA, 1986.

35. McDermott, Gerald. *Flecha al sol.* Pinguin Group, New York, 1974. Vazquez, Zoraida. *Hércules y las manzanas de oro.* Editorial Trillas. Mexico, DF, 1988.

Sixth Grade

36. Kanter, Abby, *La gran aventura de Alejandro.* Amsco School Publications. New York, 1994

Seventh and Eighth Grades

37. Alegría, Ciro. *Fábulas y leyendas Americanas.* Espasa, Madrid, séptima ed., 1997.

38. Barlow, Genevieve. *Leyendas Mexicanas.* NTC, Illinois, 1995.

39. Boy, Emily & Noguez, Susan. *Realidad y fantasía.* AMSCO, New York, 1994.

40. Bravo - Villasante, Carmen. *Antología de la literatura infantil española 1 y 2.* Editorial Doncel. Madrid, 1983.

41. Bright, M. *La deforestación tropical, nuestro mundo en peligro.* Editorial Norma S.A., Santa Fé de Bogotá, Colombia. 1993.

42. Burland, C.A. *Incas, pueblos del pasado.* Editorial Molino. Calabria, Barcelona, 1979.

43. Cabat, Louis & Robert. *Momentos hispanos.* AMSCO, New York, 1999.

44. Carrero Pérez, Luis María. *La ciudad de los dioses.* EMC Publishing. Madrid, 1991.

45. El Secreto de la Llama. Troll Associates, USA, 1993.

46. Florit, Eugenio. *Retratos de hispanoamerica.* Holt Rinehart and Winston Inc., USA, 1962.

47. Gerson, Mary. *People of Corn, a Mayan Story.* Little Brown and Co., Canada, 1995.

48. Gibbons, Jaime; Sumpter, Magdalena. *Dioses aztecas.* BES Bilingual Educational Services, INC, Los Angeles, CA, 1979.

49. Kosnik, Alice M. *Así Escribimos. A Writing Workbook for Beginning Spanish Students.* NTC. Illinois. 1993.
    - *Ya escribimos, for Advanced Beginners.* 1993.

50. Lado, R.; Adey, M.; Albini, L. *Tesoro hispánico.* McGraw Hill Book Company, New York, 1968.

51. Lasky, Kathryn. *Days of the Dead.* Hiperion Books for Children. New York, 1994.

52. McIntyre, Loren. National Geographic Society. *The Incredible Incas and their Timeless Land* Washington D.C. 1973.

53. McKissack, Patricia. *Los Incas, así es mi mundo.* Regensteiner Publishing Enterprises, Inc. USA. Children Press Chicago, 1985.

54. Palermo, Miguel Angel. *Los indios de la Pampa.* Compañía Melhoramentos de Sao Paulo, Brasil, 1993.

55. Romher, Harriet y Anchondo, Mary. *Cómo vinimos al quinto mundo.* Children BookPress. San Francisco. 1988.

56. Romher, Harriet, et al. *The Invisible Hunters / Los cazadores invisibles.* Bilingual edition. Versión en español, Zubizarreta, Roselmo & Ada, Alma Flor. Emeryville, CA: Children's Book Press, 1987.

57. Stuart, Gene and George. National Geographic Society. *Lost Kingdoms of the Maya.* Washington D.C. 1993.
    - The Mysterious Maya. 1977
    - The Mighty Aztecs. 1981

58. *The Aztecs.* Viking Division of Pinguin Books. NY, 1992.
Ugarte, Francisco. *España y su civilización.* Editorial Random House, Inc., New York. 1983.

59. Wasserman, Marvin & Carol. *Susana y Javier en Sudamérica.* AMSCO, New York, 1993.

60. Wasserman, Marvin & Carol. *Prosa moderna del mundo hispano.* AMSCO, New York, 1997.

Hispanic Biographies Series
1. Codye, Corinn. *Queen Isabella I.* Raintree Steck - Vaughn Company, Texas, 1993.

2. Gletier, Jan. *Benito Juarez.* Raintree Steck - Vaughn Company, Texas, 1993.

3. Gletier, Jan and Thompson, Katheleen. *Junípero Serra.* Raintree Steck - Vaughn Company, Texas, 1993.

4. Gletier, Jan and Thompson, Katheleen. *Simón Bolivar.* Raintree Steck - Vaughn Company, Texas, 1993.

5. Thompson, Katheleen. *Sor Juana Inés de la Cruz.* Raintree Steck - Vaughn Company, Texas, 1990.

6. Roberts, Naurice. *César Chávez y la causa.* Regensteiner Publishing Enterprises, Inc., Children Press, Chicago, 1986.

5. Resource Books for Poetry, Dramatization, and Recitation

1. Ada, Alma Flor. *A la sombra de una ala.* Editorial escuela Española, S.A. Madrid, 1988.

2. Antología poética Rubén Darío. Grupo Editorial Norma. Bogotá, Colombia, 1990.

3. Bayley, Nicola. *Canciones tontas.* Editorial Lumen.

4. Bornemann, Elsa. *Tinke Tinke.* Editorial Plus Ultra. BS. As. Argentina, 1983.
   - *Poesía infantil.* Ediciones Diman, S.R.L., Buenos Aires, 1992.
Bravo-Villasante, Carmen. *China China, Capuchina.* Editorial Susaeta. Madrid, 1981.
   - *El libro de las fábulas.* Editorial Miñón. 1973.
   - *Colorín Colorete.* Ediciones Didascalia. 1983.
De Ajo, Julia. *Mi primer libro de teatro.* Editorial Everest. Leon, España, 1988.
   - *Mi segundo libro de teatro.* 1988.

5. Garinza, Violeta. *70 canciones de aquí y de allá.* Ricordi Americana, S.A.E.C., Buenos Aires, 1967.

6. Gessler, Elizabeth. *Escenas cortas.* Gessler Publishing Co., Inc., New York, 1959.

7. Iriarte. *Fábulas de Iriarte.* Susaeta Ediciones S.A. Barcelona, España, 1973.

8. Jiménez, Juan Ramón. *Platero y Yo. Trescientos poemas.* Editorial Porrúa S.A. Mexico, 1995.

9. *Juan Ramón Jiménez para niños.* Ediciones de la Torre. Madrid, 1986.
Lorca, Federico García. *Antología poética.* Editorial Pleamar. Segunda Edición. Buenos Aires, 1943.

10. Machado, Antonio. *Poesías completas.* Editorial Espasa Calpe, S.A.. Novena Edición, Madrid, 1970.

11. Martí, José. *Los zapaticos de Rosa.* Lectorum Publications INC. New York, 1997.
   - *Ismaelillo la edad de oro de los versos sencillos.* Editorial Porrúa S.A. Mexico, 1993.

12. Medina, Arturo. *El Silvio del aire.* Selección de Arturo. Antología Juvenil 1 y 2.Editorial Vicens-vives. España, 1985.

13. Pelegrín, Ana. *Poesía española para niños.* Taurus editorial, del grupo Santillana. Madrid, 1993.

14. *Poesía española para jóvenes.* Selección de Ana Pelegrín. Alfaguara Juvenil, Madrid, 1998.

15. Sanchez Trincado, Jose Luis y Olivares Figueroa, R. *Poesía infantil recitable.* Compañia Literaria, S.L. Madrid, 1996.

16. Tarn, Nathaniel. *Pablo Neruda, Selected Poems.* Bilingual Edition. Delta Book, Dell Publishing Co., New York, 1970.

17. Versos del Montón. Poemas Latinoamericanos para Niños. Editorial Terra Nova. Mexico, 1983.

18. Vizcarrondo, Carmelina. *Campanerito azul.* Editorial Universidad De Puerto Rico, 1985.

19. Wischeussky, Amalia y Perriconi, Graciela. *La poesía infantil.* Editorial Ateneo.Argentina, 1984.

6. Resource Books for Dances, Folklore, and Various Activities

1. Brady, Agnes; Moats, Margarita. *La Navidad. Christmas in Spain and Latin America.* NTC, Illinois, 1990.

2. Candia, Antonio. *La danza folklórica en Bolivia.* Editorial Gisbert y Cía., S.A. La Paz, Bolivia. 1984.
   - *La danza folklórica en Bolivia.* Tercera Edición aumentada. 1991.

3. Carmichael, Elizabeth & Sayer, Chloe. *The Skeleton at the Feast: the Day of the Dead in Mexico.* British Museum, UK, 1991.

4. Casanova, Rogers. *Reliquias de Moxos.* Editorial Casa Municipalidad de la Cultura Franz Tamayo. Honorable Municipalidad de La Paz, Bolivia, 1977.
    - *Voces de Patití.* Librería Editorial Juventud, La Paz Bolivia. 1982.

5. Cavour, Ernesto. *La Zampoña.* Método Musical. Editorial Tatú. La Paz, Bolivia, 1974.

6. Cobo, Adrian. *Iniciación coral.* Real Música. Madrid, 1992.
Downs, Cynthia & Erickson, Gloria. *Hispanic Games & Rhymes: rimas y juegos en español.* Instructional Fair, T.S. Denison, USA, 1996.

7. De Lacré, Lulú. *Las navidades.* Editorial Scholastic Inc. New York, 1990.

8. Grasso, Dick Edgar. *Lenguas indígenas de Bolivia.* Editorial Urquizo S.A., La Paz, Bolivia, 1982.

9. Hal, *Lo mejor de nuestro folklore.* Cancionero para guitarra y charango. Producciones y Distribuiciones J. Melendres. La Paz, Bolivia, 1998.

10. Ibarra, José. (arreglados y armonizados) *Mi infancia, 30 canciones populares españolas de corro.* Editorial Música Moderna, Madrid, 1988.

11. Jurey, Edwards & Cruz, María. *Mexican Folk Dances with CD Accompaniment, Easy to Follow Dance Graphics ORFF & Percussion Arrangements.* CPP / Bewin. Miami, Florida, 1996.

12. Machicao, Porfídio. *Testificación de la Cueca.* Imprenta de la Universidad Mayor deSan Andrés, La Paz, Bolivia, 1968.

13. Medina, Arturo. *Juegos populares infantiles.* Pinto Maraña. Editorial Miñon. Valladolid, España, 1987.

14. Montoya de, Juan Hidalgo. *Cancionero infantil popular español.* Editorial Música Moderna, Madrid, España, 1990.

15. Navarro, Manuela. *Cancionero inicial E.G.B.* Ediciones SM. Madrid, 1982.

16. Orozco, José Luis. *De colores, and other Latin American Folk Songs for Children.* Dulton Children's Book. New York, 1986.
- *Fiestas - Holidays. Canciones para todo el año.* Cassette. Arco Iris Records, Berlkeley, CA, 1995.
- *Canciones de compañeros.* Shumba Productions, CA, 1985.

17. Paniagua, Rene Julio. *Historia y danzas en Mojos.* Trinidad, Beni, Bolivia, 1996.

18. Pardo, Idelfonso (armonizados y digitados) *Villancicos populares muy fáciles.* Editorial Música Moderna, Madrid, 1989.

19. Riehecky, Janet. *5 de Mayo.* Children Press, 1993.
Santiago, Esmeralda (editora) *Las Christmas: Favorite Latino Authors Share their Holiday Memories.* Alfred A. Knoph, Inc. New York, Cantomedia 1998.

20. Silverstone, Elizabeth. *Fiesta!, Mexico's Great Celebrations.* The Millbook Press, Brookfield, Connecticut, 1992.

21. The Bilingual Program of Educational Service, Center Region. *Information and Materials to Teach the Cultural Heritage of the Mexican American Children.* Bilingual Educational Services, Inc. Compiled by Minerva Gorena. Los Angeles, CA, 1986.

22. Villasante, Carmen. *Una Dola Tela Catola. El libro de folklore infantil.* Editorial Susaeta. Madrid, 1988.